AUTHOR

Giovanni Maressi (19 July 1979), pharmacist, pharmaceutical wholesaler, amateur photographer and fencing instructor, lives in Naples, capital of the Mezzogiorno. Since childhood, he has been passionate about history, especially the period between the two wars and the Second World War. Lately, he has deepened this interest by starting to carry out historical research to reconstruct his father's life and then for the present volume, which is also his second book published for Soldiershop as an author. Giovanni has also written several articles for the magazines 'Fronti di Guerra' and 'Storia & Battaglie'.

PUBLISHING'S NOTES

None of unpublished images or text of our book may be reproduced in any format without the expressed written permission of Luca Cristini Editore (already Soldiershop.com) when not indicate as marked with license creative commons 3.0 or 4.0. Luca Cristini Editore has made every reasonable effort to locate, contact and acknowledge rights holders and to correctly apply terms and conditions to Content.

Every effort has been made to trace the copyright of all the photographs. If there are unintentional omissions, please contact the publisher in writing at: info@soldiershop.com, who will correct all subsequent editions.

Our trademark: Luca Cristini Editore©, and the names of our series & brand: Soldiershop, Witness to war, Museum book, Bookmoon, Soldiers&Weapons, Battlefield, War in colour, Historical Biographies, Darwin's view, Fabula, Altrastoria, Italia Storica Ebook, Witness To History, Soldiers, Weapons & Uniforms, Storia etc. are herein © by Luca Cristini Editore.

LICENSES COMMONS

This book may utilize part of material marked with license creative commons 3.0 or 4.0 (CC BY 4.0), (CC BY-ND 4.0), (CC BY-SA 4.0) or (CC0 1.0). We give appropriate attribution credit and indicate if change were made in the acknowledgments field. Our WTW books series utilize only fonts licensed under the SIL Open Font License or other free use license.

For a complete list of Soldiershop titles please contact Luca Cristini Editore on our website: www.soldiershop.com or www.cristinieditore.com. E-mail: info@soldiershop.com

On the cover, graphic representation of the Bronze Medal for Military Valour (MBVM) awarded during the Kingdom of Italy. Above, the corresponding ribbon was blue with a bronze star in the centre.

Title: **HISTORY OF THE BLUE BARON** Code.: **WTW-052 EN** by Giovanni Maressi
ISBN code: 9791255890539 first edition December 2023
Language: English; size: 177,8x254mm Cover & Art Design: Luca S. Cristini

WITNESS TO WAR (SOLDIERSHOP) is a trademark of Luca Cristini Editore, via Orio, 35/4 - 24050 Zanica (BG) ITALY.

WITNESS TO WAR

HISTORY OF THE BLUE BARON

THE BATTLE OF MID-AUGUST AND THE CROSSING AFTER 8 SEPTEMBER

PHOTOS & IMAGES FROM WORLD WARTIME ARCHIVES

GIOVANNI MARESSI

BOOKS TO COLLECT

CONTENTS

Introduction .... Pag. 5

History of the Blue Baron .... Pag. 9

Attacking aircraft crews of 12 August 1942 .... Pag. 56

Fallen of the Regia Aeronautica .... Pag. 57

Photo album .... Pag. 58

Bibliography .... Pag. 95

▲ An S. 79S (torpedo version) pictured on the cover of the supplement to 'Le vie dell'aria' entitled *Aerei italiani contro navi inglesi (Italian aircraft against British ships)*, (photo g.c. Collezione Bruno Fochesato, op. cit. in bibliography).

INTRODUCTION

My uncle, Carlo Winspeare

by Edoardo Winspeare

Who was Carlo Winspeare? Why write about his life? As his nephew, son of his brother Riccardo, I would not be the best person to give a comprehensive and detached answer, but I believe that having grown up in the same family as his 'good and crazy' uncle, where the myth of his originality was constantly fed by his exploits, can contribute to restoring an idea of the character, albeit a partial one.

The youngest of the Winspeare brothers was kind and good-natured, had a dreamy disposition and great mathematical talent, but at the same time went through moments of madness. His relatives called him 'the original', but nevertheless bet on his precocious intelligence, hoping for a brilliant scientific career for him. For the rest of his life, however, he remained an eccentric idealist, an emulation of St Francis who, with childlike candour, hoped that the Earth would once again become an Eden of peace and love. He preached goodness and practised charity, at every opportunity and with missionary zeal. With all this, his radical choices, even if made for good, overwhelmed the lives of those close to him, for better or for worse. In any case, I adored him as a child, because he also remained a child, and everything was turned into an adventure by him. The death of his father was a terrible blow for the barely adolescent Carletto, as he was called by everyone. He was the darling of Rear Admiral Edoardo Winspeare, both because of a parent's natural sense of protection for the youngest of his children, who had already been motherless since the age of two, and also because of their shared interest in science and curiosity about every new invention. Uncle Carlo had been a man of extremes since childhood. He was able to build a radio transmitter or a television set with his own hands, but felt the need to go to mass every day; unlike his brother Riccardo, who was a very secular Catholic, influenced by the Protestantism of his mother's Danish-American family and went through moments of agnostic doubts. In Uncle Carlo, a positivist nature coexisted (he took two degrees, in Biological Sciences and in Mathematics, where he was a pupil, among others, of Renato Caccioppoli, whom he admired above all for his intelligence and charisma), and a mystical soul. He had participated in the construction of great works such as the Monte Vergine transmitter centre, had published scientific articles and translated texts on the same subject from English, and at the same time worshipped women in the odour of sanctity who fed solely on the consecrated host. He was also a fervent devotee of Padre Pio, from whom he sometimes received a few slaps during their tormented confessions. But it did not end there. Among his many extravagances was nudism, which Uncle Carlo had been practising on the beach since the 1930s. Imagine the scandal among bathers in southern Italy at that time. Dad used to tell me that in Sicily he had to chase him all along the beach at Mazzarò, with his towel and his costume in hand, to convince him to cover up. During the war, he fought as a lieutenant pilot in Commander Buscaglia's torpedo bomber squadron. He was a daredevil, decorated with two bronze medals for military valour. He received his first decoration for his participation in the sinking of a British ship in the Mediterranean. As chance would have it, forty years later, I had his marconist as a maths teacher in high school. When, on the first day of school, Professor Mici - that was his name - scrolled through the list of students with his head bent over the register, read my surname, looked up and, seriously, asked me if I was related to Commander Carlo Winspeare. When he got confirmation that I was his nephew, he promised me years of hell. He told me that his uncle was a madman who would only release the torpedo when the torpedo bomber was very close to the enemy ship, ignoring the terrified screams of the crew members who were begging him to regain altitude to escape the close anti-aircraft gunfire. In my naivety as a teenager, I actually thought that, almost half a century later, the professor was trying to make me pay for my uncle's reckless ventures. Luckily he was joking, and on the contrary, he always promoted me 'for war merits', despite the fact that I was a disaster in mathematics, such was his esteem and affection for his pilot commander. I also believe that later on, after an initial period of warlike enthusiasm, Uncle had suffered a very strong shock; I do not know whether on one specific occasion or because he had opened his eyes to the true face of war. The fact is that, from a certain moment on, he decided that he would never again kill a human being. To be true to this vow, when he was on a mission over the Mediterranean, he would fire his torpedoes into the sea before reaching the enemy target. It is a good story, albeit an incredible one. Whether true, false or exaggerated, this is what he wanted us to know about his combat experience. I imagine that facing death every day sent him into a deep crisis that must have haunted him until the end of his life. Who knows if his excessive actions were not a way of exorcising death. For many years after the war, he tempted fate by flying small touring planes with half-empty fuel tanks, for the gamble of landing with the engines off once the fuel ran out. Uncle Carlo's perception of events went from a lucid analysis of objective reality to a hallucinated distortion of events, and the border between the two ways of seeing was never defined. I know with certainty that he refused to drop bombs on Valletta - which, not coincidentally, was the city where he was born - and perhaps this was the triggering episode for his conversion to pacifism. At the armistice of 8 September, as a loyal monarchist, he decided to continue serving King Victor Emmanuel III, who in the meantime had taken refuge in the South liberated by the Anglo-Americans. In those days, Uncle Carlo was hiding in German-occupied northern Italy, with the risk, if discovered, of being deported to Germany. To reach the south, he stole a German patrol boat in a port in the Marche region. For this feat he was decorated with a second bronze medal.

Uncle Carlo continued the war on intelligence missions with the British *A-Force* beyond the Gustav Line. Countess Andreola Vinci's diary tells of the gentle and poetic Carlo Winspeare, with a face of a boy not yet of age and a head so in the clouds - at least in appearance - that he would hardly have attracted the suspicions of the Nazi-Fascists. There is an episode in the book *'The Buscaglia Group'*, written by his military valour gold medal-winning comrade Martino Aichner, that sums up Uncle Carlo's romantic and spiritual soul well. A British Hurricane fighter plane had been shot down by Italian anti-aircraft fire on the torpedo bomber airfield in Sicily. Lieutenant Winspeare, who knew English perfectly, had been sent by Commander Buscaglia to check the enemy pilot's papers. Receiving no news from ours for a long time, the commander ordered Aichner himself to go and check what was going on. When the fellow pilot reached Uncle Carlo in front of the Hurricane's carcass, he found him absorbed in prayer. It was only then that his uncle interrupted, translated the dead young Englishman's identification card and handed it to him wrapped in a sheet of paper where he had written these verses by Thomas Gray: 'Here *rests his head upon the* lap of Earth / *A youth* to Fortune *and to Fame unknown*'. After the war, Uncle Carlo campaigned for the 1946 referendum with sometimes excessive ardour in favour of the monarchy. He also ended up in prison following some clashes with supporters of the republic. However, when he met a poor person he would take off his coat and give it to them, or he would take out all the money he had and distribute it to those in need (or those who took advantage of him). If his brother Riccardo organised a party at Villa Salve with the best names in Naples, Uncle Carlo went to the working-class neighbourhoods, to Sanità, Pallonetto or Forcella, inviting people who had probably never been to Vomero or Posillipo. In 1946 he had married Maria Vittoria Colonna di Stigliano, an angel of a woman, elegant and distinguished, who had agreed to become his wife even though she knew he was sterile, due to a venereal disease contracted during the war. Aunt Vittoria, more than a consort, was for his uncle the mother he never knew. And she loved him tenderly as one loves a wild child, whose brilliance one admires and forgives him every morning, even when he was up to no good, as when he left her for a Mexican 'holy woman'. On that occasion, the aunt, who had never flown a plane, flew to Mexico to take back her husband who was in love with the Mayan mystic. But his masterpiece of radicalism was that he abandoned his wife to live with and assist a woman who had in the Eucharist her only nourishment, of course after giving, in imitation of the Saint of Assisi, everything he had. The problem was that the Winspeare brothers' property was still undivided, which led to years of lawyers and court cases to establish the division with Dad, and a survival share for his wife. To make matters worse, poor Aunt Vittoria, after being left by Uncle Carlo overnight, was refused a divorce for twenty years because it went against her husband's Christian morals. I must say that on dad's side I never perceived any animosity towards his brother, only sadness and certainly some regret for how he had liquidated such a beautiful property. Aunt Vittoria on the other hand, who had not seen her husband since 1977 - since he had moved to Cavriago near Reggio Emilia -, always felt enormous affection for her Carlo until his last days in 2010. Some tragicomic anecdotes from his life, which any wife would have remembered with anger, were recounted by Aunt Vittoria with amused indulgence, *"you know, he was like that..."* Once, just after the war, during a trip in a Lambretta from Naples to Messina, after a stop for petrol, Uncle Carlo had left, forgetting his wife at the service station, and continuing unnoticed all the way to Sicily. After quite a while, Aunt Vittoria finally managed to talk to him by phoning their house in Messina, but Uncle Carlo had forgotten all about it in the meantime, in fact he was so worried about not finding her that he said to her: *"But where have you gone all this time?!"* Aunt Vittoria always managed to justify it. When very old, now in her nineties, she heard my footsteps approaching her room in our house in Depressa, where she had eventually moved from Naples, she would ask in a voice broken with anxiety, *"Are you Carlo?"*, thus betraying a desire to see him again. In short, Uncle Carlo was an original man, full of contradictions and fundamentally good. And this is how I want to remember him.

▲ Admiral Edoardo Winspeare (02.02.1875-26.05.1931) travelled the world in the retinue of Luigi Amedeo di Savoia, the adventurous Duke of the Abruzzi, serving as *attaché militaire*, as an officer of the Regia Marina, at the diplomatic representation of the Kingdom of Italy in Malta, when his son Carlo was born (photo g.c. Collezione Edoardo Winspeare).

HISTORY OF THE BLUE BARON
The Battle of Mid-August and the crossing after 8 September

To Maria Vittoria Colonna "Ba".

Carlo Luigi Amedeo Winspeare Guicciardi[1] the son of Edoardo and Clara Sarauw[2] was born on 13 March 1917 in Valletta (Malta) where his father, who had already travelled the world in the retinue of Luigi Amedeo di Savoia, the adventurous Duke of the Abruzzi, was an *attaché militaire*, as an officer in the Royal Navy. Enrolled in the conscription lists of the City of Naples (where he was domiciled at Via S. Stefano 4, Vomero Vecchio), he belonged to the Military District of Naples as a revisable conscript of the class of 1917. Left on unlimited leave on 2 May 1938, he had to answer the call to arms with the class of 1918. Called to arms on 29 March 1939, 'ours' was admitted to delay military service for study reasons, as he was enrolled in the first year at the Faculty of Natural Sciences at the Royal University of Naples 'Federico II'. On 1 December 1939, he was incorporated into the Regia Aeronautica (Royal Air Force), after being removed from the Regio Esercito (Royal Army) rolls with serial number 629578, as a trainee pilot airman in order to complete his military service, because he held a civil pilot's licence of the 1st grade (initially, holders of civil licences were called to arms with the rank of second lieutenant *N.d.A.*), in the Lever and Recruitment Centre of the 4ª Territorial Air Zone (ZAT) in Benevento[3]. He was then sent on temporary unlimited leave, while waiting to be sent to a pilot school to obtain a military pilot's licence. On 7 December 1939, he was awarded the rank of first airman cadet pilot officer with seniority from 1 December 1939 and starting from the date of his return from said leave. On 5 February 1940 he was recalled from leave and sent to the 1st Period Pilot School at the Royal Airport of Perugia Sant'Egidio. On 11 June 1940 he was mobilised to a territory declared to be in a state of war and a zone of operations. Appointed aeroplane pilot on Ro. 41 aircraft on 5 September 1940, on 9 September 1940 he was transferred to the Aviano Pilot School. He obtained his pilot's licence to fly the S. 81 «Pipistrello» on 29 December 1940 (effective 26 December 1940) at the Royal Air Force School in Aviano. In addition, he was qualified to pilot the Ca. 313 from 6 January 1941, as per communication from the command of the 3ª Air Squadron (Rome). Appointed military pilot on the S. 79 «Sparrowhawk» three-engine multi-role low-wing aircraft (also known as the «cursed hump» due to the typical hump behind the cockpit that housed the Breda-SAFAT 12.7 mm machine guns in the fighter and dorsal plus the gunner *N.d.A.*) *as of* 23 May 1941 (qualification obtained on 29 March

---

1 The surname Winspeare means (man *N.A.*) by the winning spear being composed of the words *'win'* and *'spear'*. The lineage, originally from Glaisdale, Whitby in Yorkshire, split into two branches in the 19th century and became part of the aristocracy thanks to the title of baron awarded by Joachim Murat with Royal Decree of 17.12.1814. The family was recognised by the Italian government with a Ministerial Decree of 20.03.1917, reconfirmed, with sovereign concession *motu proprio*, on 17.08.1942. The Winspeare family were sanctioned during the Second World War because of their surname of English origin, and it did not take long for the authorities to realise that they were making a mistake. The exponents of one of the two branches were authorised, by Royal Decree of 14.01.1943, to add the surname Guicciardi : during the war, it was convenient to have an Italian surname next to the English 'enemy' one.

2 Sicilian noblewoman of Danish-American origin (08.04.1883-05.02.1919).

3 The Recruitment and Mobilisation Centre for 3ª ZAT was transferred on 25 July 1928 from Capua to Benevento at the 'Caserma Sannitica', which, the following year, would be named after General Alessandro Guidoni, the father of the torpedo bomber. On 1 July 1935, this centre was in operation for the 4ª ZAT. The Benevento military airfield in contrada Olivola (which from 1940 fell within the area of the 4ª Air Squadron) was used during the Second World War as a repair and test workshop for the Savoia Marchetti S. 79 'Sparviero'.

▲ In the centre, standing on the bench, Carlo Winspeare as a child clasps a bell in his left hand; the soldier on his right is his cousin, Count Francesco Cicogna Mozzoni 'Pato', who was a lieutenant (see the rank insignia, two stars, sewn onto the wrists of his open-necked jacket with black insignia, typical of the Arditi) in the mountain artillery complement during the period 1915-1918 (photo g.c. Collection Edoardo Winspeare).

1941 at the Regia Aeronautica School in Aviano), he was held at arms on 6 August 1941 for the completion of his training. On 25 July 1941, he was promoted to second lieutenant in the Air Force, sailor role, and assigned to the Bombardment School or to the 2nd Aircraft Training Unit[4] in Capodichino (NA) with administrative effect from the date of his presentation to the corps where he arrived on 6 September 1941. Thus, the director of courses at the Aviano School, Major Pilot Mingardo Jagos, drew up the information report dated 15 September 1941 on Carlo Winspeare at the end of his training cycle:

[...] Second Lieutenant A.A.r.n. Complement Pilot WINSPEARE Carlo served at this school from 13 September 1940 to 5 September 1941, as 1st Airman All. Pilot. He obtained his military licence and war training in the B.T. (Land Bombardment N.d.A.) speciality on S. 81 and S. 79 aircraft. He re-

▲ The Winspeare Guicciardi coat of arms (photo g.c. Collegio Heraldico Collection).

vealed good qualities as a pilot with special aptitude for multi-engine aircraft. He displayed passion, enthusiasm, and flight discipline. Not many brilliant results in theoretical exams and practical exercises. Of good health, not very robust, almost gives the impression that he must be ill, but instead withstands the hardships of flight and military life very well. Of distinguished appearance, slender build, devotes himself to sports in general, knows how to swim. Of excellent moral, patriotic and fascist sentiments, he has an open willingness to learn. Of a rather closed character, not very lively, does not like company much. He does not have much of a vocation for military life, he is not overzealous in carrying out the tasks entrusted to him. His reasoning is balanced, good memory, expresses himself clearly. His general education is good, sufficient for his rank. A very young element, he has little command authority and little influence over his inferiors. With superiors he is very respectful, good comradeship with colleagues. He needs to study in order to improve and perfect his technical and professional knowledge. Discipline-wise, his behaviour has not given reason for significant reprimands. He is sufficiently familiar with the equipment, installations, *and* instruments on board the S. 81 and S. 79 aircraft (AUSAM, Personal Documentation Fund, Personal Booklet Series, Personal Booklet of Pilot Winspeare Carlo).

---

4 The 1st Aerosilent Training Unit was established in Gorizia, while the 3rd Aerosilent Training Unit was based in Pisa. [...] The training concerned exclusively the specific employment: pendulum over the sea, target identification, study of the best approach route, launch route, release and escape phase. The torpedo had to be launched from an altitude of less than 100 m, at a speed of 300 km/h. All this in the midst of the extremely violent anti-aircraft fire, to which the big guns were often added, raising high columns on the water (the 'fountains', also due to bombs dropped by friendly aircraft, could reach up to 100 m in height), an insidious additional obstacle (together with the 'combs' of the ships' machine guns that tried to intercept and detonate the torpedoes, *Ed.*) Between late 1940 and late 1941, seven squadrons were formed, numbered in order from 278ª to 284ª. Then the units reached the consistency of four flocks and 12 groups, with varying permanence in the specialty (AA.VV., Nei Cieli di Guerra, La Regia Aeronautica a colori 1940-45, Milano, Giorgio Apostolo Editore, 1996).

He was paid, by the Administrative Office of the Royal Airport in Aviano (No. 241, PM 3200), half of the campaign entry allowance of 2,000 Lire gross (908 Lire net) on 27 September 1941. On 23 February 1942, he took the oath of allegiance at Capodichino. He graduated[5] in Natural Sciences on 26 February 1942 from the Royal University of Naples. He took part in war operations on the Mediterranean front from 25 April 1942 to 10 December 1942 and from 19 January 1943 to 14 July 1943, for which he was entitled to two campaigns (1942-1943) of war. On 29 April 1942, he was at 281ª Squadron of the 132nd Autonomous Aerosilhouette Group[6] (the wording 281ª Squadron appears crossed out in the service record *N.d.A.*). From 7 June 1942 to 22 June 1942 he was on a 15-day premium leave, granted by the Air Force Command of Sicily. On 27 June 1942 he was paid, by the Administrative Office of the Royal Airport of Gerbini[7] (CT) the gross sum of 2,304 lire as the amount for 30 days of leave not taken during the year (from 11.06.1941 to 10.06.1942). Carlo Winspeare's nephew, the well-known director Edoardo, reports an episode (dating back to this period *N.d.A.*):

[...] In the book 'The Buscaglia Group', written by his comrade-in-arms, Gold Medalist for Military Valour Martino Aichner[8], which sums up Uncle Carlo's romantic and spiritual soul well. A British Hurricane fighter plane had been shot down by Italian anti-aircraft fire on the torpedo bomber airfield in Sicily. Lieutenant Winspeare, who knew English perfectly, had been sent by Commander Buscaglia[9] to check the enemy pilot's papers. Receiving no news from ours for a long time, the commander ordered Aichner himself to go and check

---

5 He also obtained a second degree in mathematics and was a student of Professor Renato Caccioppoli (1904-1959), a great Neapolitan mathematician, whom he admired for his intelligence and charisma. In 1931, Caccioppoli won the chair of Algebraic Analysis at the University of Padua. In 1934 he returned to Naples to hold the chair of Group Theory, then moved on to the chair of Higher Analysis and, from 1943, to that of Mathematical Analysis. In 1947 he became a member of the Accademia dei Lincei and, in 1953, the same Academy awarded him the National Prize for Physical, Mathematical and Natural Sciences. His most important studies, some eighty publications, concern functional analysis and the calculus of variations. Disappointments in politics (after the war he approached the Italian Communist Party), the fading of his mathematical vein and the abandonment of his wife led him to alcoholism. On 8 May 1959, he took his own life with a pistol shot in his home at the Palazzo Cellammare.

6 The 281ª Autonomous Aerosailor Squadron was born in Grottaglie (TA) under the command of Capt. Carlo Emanuele Buscaglia on 5 March 1941 and was transferred to Gadurrà on the island of Rhodes. On 1 April 1942, the 281ª Squadron, together with the 278ª Squadron, formed the 132nd Autonomous Aerosilhouette Group (as ordered by the Command of the 3ª Air Squadron, sheet no. 031491/S of 31.03.1942), based in Littoria (today Latina *N.d.A.*), under the command of Buscaglia who was later promoted to Major. The 281ª Squadron, based at Littoria Airport, then passed under the command of Capt. Giulio Cesare Graziani, nephew of Marshal Rodolfo of Italy. Instead, the headquarters of 278ª Squadron was based at Castelvetrano Airport (TP). Later, the 281ª Squadron was transferred to Sicily, at Fontanarossa Airport (CT). As of 01.04.1942, the flying personnel consisted of: 21 pilots (11 officers and 10 non-commissioned officers); 46 specialists (16 motorists, 9 fitters, 8 marconists, 11 gunners and 2 photographers). Ours' arrived on 29.04.1942 at 281ª Squadron, when the 132nd Group was only 2 days away, which explains the cancellation.

7 In 1942, the command nucleus of the 132nd Autonomous Aero Group was based at Gerbini Sud (PM 3500) airfield No. 505, in the Catania plain at the foot of Mount Etna. Also belonging to the Gerbini base were the satellite camps of San Salvatore (Scordia), Finocchiara, Sigonella and Spina Santa. During the Allied invasion, from July 1943, the base was occupied by Anglo-American troops who used its runways for their advance towards the continent.

8 This is the dedication that Martino Aichner wrote on the copy of his book given to Carlo Winspeare:
To my friend Carlo Winspeare with the deepest feeling for the long-standing friendship born in the flying school.
Affectionately, Martino
February 1981

9 Carlo Emanuele Buscaglia was born on 22 September 1915 in Novara. He was one of the most famous Italian aviators of World War II. Believed dead in the Bougie roadstead after a torpedoing action, he was decorated with the Gold Medal for Military Valour. The command of the 132nd Group, which on 14.11.1942 (5113/C Stataereo Catania) assumed the name 'Carlo Emanuele Buscaglia Group', passed to Graziani and was then entrusted to Major Gabriele Casini. On 23 August 1944, Buscaglia attempted to take off, without authorisation, with a *Baltimore* bomber from Campo Vesuvio. However, the aircraft lifted off the ground too early, yawed as its left wing touched the runway and caught fire. Buscaglia, burnt and injured, managed to get away from the aircraft, was rescued and admitted to the British military hospital in Naples, but, unfortunately, died the following day.

▲ Hangar and destroyed aircraft at the Benevento military airport used during World War II as a repair and test workshop for the Savoia-Marchetti S. 79 'Sparviero' (photo taken from https://catalog.archives.gov/).

what was going on. When the fellow pilot reached Uncle Carlo in front of the Hurricane's carcass, he found him absorbed in prayer. Only at that point did his uncle interrupt, translate to him the identification card of the dead young Englishman (he was *sergeant* Webster[10], probably shot down by airport *anti-aircraft* fire) and hand it to him wrapped in a sheet of paper where he had written these verses (taken from Elegy Written in a Country Churchyard *N.d.A.*) by Thomas Gray: «Here rests his head upon the lap of *Earth* / A *youth* to Fortune and to Fame unknown» (transl. it. «*Qui giace nel grembo della nuda terra / Un giovane sconosciuto alla gloria e alla fortuna terrena*») (Winspeare, Edoardo, Extract on Uncle Carlo).

Now let us see why the 132nd Group was stationed in Sicily. Already at the beginning of 1942, the Prime Minister of the United Kingdom noted that:

---

10 According to the Commonwealth War Graves Commission (CWGC), in the time span from 01.04.1942 to 31.08.1942, *Sgt* Frank Webster Tregear (RAAF 402893) died on 24.04.1942 while strafing an enemy motorised transport column. After the attack, passing over the target, a truck exploded and the aircraft was seen crashing in flames. Following post-war searches and investigations, no trace of the plane or the missing pilot was found. His name is remembered on column 266 at the Alamein Memorial in Egypt. Instead, *Sgt* (*observer*) William White Webster (RAF VR 1100851) died on 13.06.1942, at the end of an air test. The pilot of the plane he was in apparently decided to 'hit' the aerodrome, but stalled vertically. The aircraft crashed into the roof of a car which was being driven by *Wt Off* F K G Relton of 601 Sqdn who was killed along with the pilot J P Doncaster and his observer. His name is commemorated at the Malta (Capuccini) Naval Cemetery. In the first case, the name, the rank, the date of the crash and the aircraft (*Kittyhawk II*, serial number: AK 966) correspond to Aichner's description, but not the department he belonged to (260 Sqdn Middle East) and the place of the crash (Cyrenaica, Libya). In the second case, the surname, the rank, the department (235 Sqdn) and the date of the crash might match Aichner's description, but not the aircraft (*Beaufighter*, serial number: T5006/P) and the crash site (Hal Far, Malta).

▲ S. Egidio Airport (PG) July/December 1941, swearing in of cadet sergeants No. 900 "University Battalion" (photo g.c. Giancarlo Faltoni Collection).

[...] At the moment the Mediterranean is closed to us and all our transport ships are forced to circumnavigate the Cape of Good Hope, which only allows them to complete three voyages in the course of the year. All our ships, our aeroplanes, our tanks, and all our anti-tank and anti-aircraft guns are currently in action. Everything we have has been deployed against the enemy, or for protection against possible attack by the enemy (Message from Prime Minister Winston Churchill on the state of the conflict, broadcast over the radio on 15 February 1942).

Having failed the *Harpoon* (from Gibraltar) and *Vigorous* (from Alexandria) operations, two simultaneous convoys sent to resupply Malta, from which the Battle of Pantelleria or Mid-June took place, for two months, lacking the possibility of attacking British ships that did not sail the Central Mediterranean, the Air Force Command of Sicily employed the 132nd Group to protect the convoys that from Italy resupplied the North African front. These were the times of the conquest of Tobruch and the advance to El Alamein. Meanwhile, the *Royal Navy* assembled a powerful new fleet to counter the Axis naval blockade of the Malta stronghold. On 10 August 1942, an impressive naval squadron crossed the Strait of Gibraltar (which was spotted by a Spanish merchant ship on the opposite route and a civilian aircraft bound for Algeria), a movement that did not escape the Italian-German agents present in Spain, commanded by *Vice Admiral* Edward Neville Syfret . It was divided into the following Forces: F (Force as a whole), Z (Force F minus Force X), X (escort, commanded by *RAdm* Harold Martin Burrough of the 10th Cruiser Squadron), Y (convoy and escort with Italian insignia from Malta to Gibraltar, called Operation *Ascendant*) and R (fleet consisting of 2 tankers, 4 escort corvettes and 1 tug). E formata da 4 portaerei, la *HMS Eagle* (*Capt* Lachlan Donald Mackintosh), la *HMS Furious* (*Capt* Tom Oliver Bulteel), la *HMS Victorious* (*Capt* Henry Cecil Bovell, nave di bandiera del comandante delle portaerei, *RAdm* Arthur Lumley St. George Lyster, Fifth Sea Lord) and *HMS Indomitable* (*Capt*

▲ Carlo Winspeare was appointed aeroplane pilot on the IMAM Ro. 41 fighter and training aircraft as of 9 September 1940 (photo Fortepan, taken from https://commons.wikimedia.org/).

▼ Carlo Winspeare photographed next to a FIAT B.R.20 'Stork' aircraft (note the drawing on the fuselage of Donald Duck, a Walt Disney character, irritatedly raising his sleeve, the symbol of the 1st Terrestrial Bombardment Squadron). From the mountains in the background, it appears that the location of the shot is the Aviano airfield (photo g.c. Collezione Edoardo Winspeare).

▲ Barracks building, at the Aviano (PN) airport, damaged by bombs (photo taken from https://catalog.archives.gov/).

▼ Carlo Winspeare qualified to fly the Savoia-Marchetti S. 81 'Pipistrello' bomber on 29 December 1940 (photo Charles Daniel's Collection Italian Aircraft Album, taken from https://flickr.com/).

▲ Carlo Winspeare was qualified as pilot on Caproni 313 reconnaissance and light bomber aircraft from 6 January 1941 (photo taken from *Catalogo Nomenclatore per Aeroplano Caproni 313 da Ricognizione e medio Bombardamento*, op. cit. in bibliography).

▼ SIAI Savoia-Marchetti type S. 79 "Sparviero" on display at the Museo Storico dell'Aeronautica Militare in Vigna di Valle (RM), the wing cockades consisting of three stylised lictor fasces inscribed in a circle and the torpedo at the bottom are clearly visible. The aircraft was produced in about 1,200 examples in the military bomber and torpedo bomber versions with MM. between 21051 and 25395. Second Lieutenant Winspeare was appointed military pilot on this aircraft as of 23 May 1941 (photo Maurizio Barber via G. Maressi).

Thomas Hope Troubridge), on which 138 aircraft (46 *Sea Hurricane*, 10 *Martlet*, 16 *Fulmar*, 38 *Spitfire* and 28 *Albacore*) were embarked; 2 battleships, HMS *Nelson* (*Capt* Humphrey Benson Jacomb, flagship of *VAdm* Edward Neville Syfret) and HMS *Rodney* (*Capt* James William Rivett-Carnac), 7 cruisers (*HMS Nigeria, HMS Kenya, HMS Manchester, HMS Phoebe, HMS Charybdis, HMS Sirius, HMS Cairo*), 32 destroyers (*Capt* Reginald Maurice James Hutton of the 19ª Destroyer Flotilla and *Acting Capt* Richard George Onslow of the 6ª Destroyer Flotilla), 8 submarines and other smaller vessels that were to protect the convoy *W.S.21S.*[11], which sailed from Clyde on 3 August. This consisted of 13 merchant ships [*MV Empire Hope, SS Dorset, MV Wairangi, SS Rochester Castle, MV Waimarama, MV Brisbane Star, SS Port Chalmers, SS Almeria Lykes (US), SS Santa Elisa (US), SS Clan Ferguson, MV Glenorchy, MV Melbourne Star, SS Deucalion*] and 1 tanker (*SS Ohio* of the Texas Company) loaded with provisions, fuel, and war material. Normally, W.S. convoys were those from the UK to Suez via the Cape of Good Hope, but this was Operation *Pedestal*, known in Malta as *Il-Konvoj ta' Santa Marija* because it was scheduled to arrive on Saturday 15 August on the feast of the Assumption of Mary, or simply *The Malta Convoy* for the British. Initially it was planned to take off from Gibraltar the 38 *Spitfires* to be delivered to Malta (Operation *Bellows*) of which 36 arrived at their destination:

[...] Sir Dudley Pound (Admiral of the Fleet and First Sea Lord N.*d.A.*) stated that it would not be necessary to arrange other elements for the flight of the next squadron of Spitfires to Malta. Sir Charles Portal (Air Marshal and Chief of Staff of the RAF N.A.A.) stated that an attempt could be made to fly the aircraft directly from Gibraltar, provided the wind was favourable and he accepted the risk of crash landings in Tunisia. He then indicated that he would look into the matter and get in touch with the First Lord of the Admiralty (Albert Victor Alexander *Ed.*) that same evening... (National Archives Kew, War Cabinet. Chiefs Of Staff Committee. Minutes of Meeting held on Tuesday, 11st August, 1942, at 5.45 p.m.).

Then it was decided that the planes would be embarked on HMS *Furious*, which would reverse course at Algiers, once these had taken off. The combined action of the Regia Aeronautica and the *Luftwaffe* proved deadly for the huge convoy.

▲ Photographic portrait of Regia Aeronautica's second lieutenant pilot Carlo Winspeare, note the pilot's badge (an eagle, resting on a fascio littorio, looking to the right surmounted by the crown of the Royal House of Savoy) above the row of ribbons and the pair of lower officer's rafters of the navigating role on the respective shoulders of the uniform (photo g.c. Collezione Edoardo Winspeare).

---

11 W.S. convoys, as a rule, were those heading from the UK to Suez via the Cape of Good Hope.

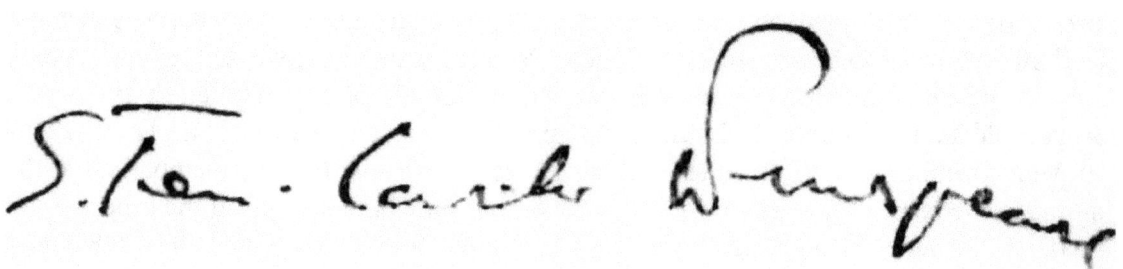
▲ The signature of Regia Aeronautica second lieutenant Carlo Winspeare (author photo).

Supermarina, being short of fuel, did not deploy the costly battleships but instead employed the cruisers Bolzano (C.V. Mario Mezzadra), Gorizia (C.V. Paolo Melodia, Adm. Angelo Parona's flagship), Trieste (C.V. Umberto Rouselle) of the 3ª Naval Division from Messina; Muzio Attendolo (C.V. Mario Schiavuta), Eugenio di Savoia (C. V. Franco Zannoni, flagship of Adm.V. Franco Zannoni, Admiral Alberto Da Zara's flagship) and Raimondo Montecuccoli (C. V. Arturo Solari) of the 7ª Naval Division coming from Cagliari (except for the Attendolo out of Naples), 6 motor torpedo boats (MS), 13 Mas and 18 submarines, these naval divisions were under the command of Admirals Angelo Parona and Alberto Da Zara respectively. The *Kriegsmarine* deployed 2 submarines (*U-Boot*) and 4 motor torpedo boats (*S-Boot*). Great reliance was placed on minefields in the waters near the Sicilian Channel, such as the temporary barrage 'S.t. 1', laid by the destroyer Lanzerotto Malocello, on 10 August 1942. On the eve of the battle, Superaereo had 328 aircraft in Sardinia and Sicily, while the *Luftwaffe* had 456 aircraft. The *Royal Air Force* (RAF), on the other hand, deployed 141 aircraft (increased to 186 on 14 August). Unlike in June, it was decided to send from Port Said, in the eastern Mediterranean, a 'diversionary Malta convoy' named M.W.12 (Operation M.G. 3) that would meet another similar convoy coming from Haifa, in order to split the Italian-German air force. The British would not be unprepared:

> [...] Sir Charles Portal referred to signals that had been exchanged between the V.A. (Vice Admiral) in Malta and the Admiralty about possible interference by the enemy with Operation «PEDESTAL» and distributed in his own hand to all copies of a draft of a telegram concerning support from heavy bombers and torpedo bombers for this Operation. (National Archives Kew, War Cabinet. Chiefs Of Staff Committee. Minutes of Meeting held on Friday, 31st July, 1942, at 10.30 a.m.).

On 11 August 1942, the convoy was sighted at 04.38 by the Italian submarine Uarscieck (T.V. Gaetano Arezzo della Targia), but the news did not reach Rome until 10.25, and by a Ju. 88 of 1. (F) *Aufklärungsgruppe* 122 which had departed from Elmas (CA). The aircraft was damaged by *Sea Hurricanes* from the flight deck of HMS *Indomitable* (which, having just taken part in Operation *Berserk*, a joint carrier exercise, was mistaken for the USS *Wasp, Ed.*), but it was able to accurately communicate the enemy's coordinates at 08.15 hours (10.10 hours according to Italian documentation, *Ed.*) and returned with dead and wounded on board. The Battle of Mid-August had just begun. The 132nd Autonomous Aerosilurant Group was finalising its preparations for action: 'Eight S. 79 aircraft of 278ª Squadron and seven of 281ª Squadron move (from Gerbini *N.d.A.*) by torpedo to Pantelleria Airport (equipped with a large hangar dug out of the rock *N.d.A.*) and remained there on alert' (AUSAM, Fondo Diari Storici Seconda Guerra Mondiale 1940-1945, Serie anno 1942, fascicolo 897, 132nd Gruppo Aerosiluranti , 9-15 August 1942). And, 'three S. 79

aircraft of the 278ᵃ Squadron and three of the 281ᵃ Squadron from Pantelleria returned to Gerbini for torpedo pick-up and returned to Pantelleria during the day' (op. cit.). At 1.15 p.m., 4 torpedoes launched by the German submarine U-73, commanded by the not yet 30-year old *kapitänleutnant* Helmut Rosenbaum, hit the aircraft carrier *HMS Eagle* (22,200 t)[12] which sank in about 8 minutes with all 12 *Sea Hurricanes* that were embarked at that moment, the remaining 4 that were on patrol at that time landed later on the other aircraft carriers[13]. At sunset, from 20.10 to 21.35 on 11 August, 9 *Beaufighter* aircraft of 248 *Squadron*, under the command of Lieutenant Colonel Thomas Geoffrey Pike, coming from Malta and taking off from Luqa airport, caused the death of 2 servicemen and the wounding of 4 others, destroyed 5 S. 79 and 1 Ca. 164 and damaged 18 others (of which 14 S.79, 2 S. 84s and 2 Re. 2001s) parked at bases in the Cagliari area (Elmas and Decimomannu); 3 German Macchi C 202s and 3 Bf 109s should also be added to the tally of damaged aircraft. During the night, other aircraft, including two B-24 *Liberators* from the Middle East operating from Malta, flew over Villacidro airport and the bases already mentioned, but the action failed. In the meantime, the British fleet was moving away from the Sardinian Air Force area, falling, from mid-afternoon, into the range of the Italian Air Force and *Luftwaffe* units based in Sicily. The following day, Wednesday 12 August, 'two S. 79 aircraft of the 281ᵃ Squadron moved to Pantelleria Airport, returning there on alert' (op. cit.). From here, at 17.30 hours, 14 S. 79 «Sparviero» aircraft took to the air, with excellent visibility and weather conditions. 79 «Sparviero»[14] (7 aircraft of the 278ᵃ Squadron and 7 aircraft of the 281ᵃ Squadron) of the 16 scheduled to take part in the action, commanded *ad interim* by Captain Ugo Rivoli from Pula (Buscaglia, who had been promoted to Major, was on a leave of absence in continental Italy where he visited barracks and schools between Rome, Milan and Novara) and 9 Ju. 87 «Picchiatello» fighters (transferred from Gela) of the 102ⁿᵈ Group under Captain Antonio Cumbat. Escorting them were 28 Macchi C 202 'Folgore' fighters from the 51ˢᵗ Terrestrial Fighter Wing commanded by Lieutenant Colonel Aldo Remondino: 17 from Major Duilio Fanali's 155ᵗʰ Group and 11 from Major Gino Callieri's 20ᵗʰ Group. The Germans arrived from Trapani with 20 Ju. 87 *Stuka* of the I. *Sturzkampfgeschwader* 3, commanded by *Hauptmann* Martin Mussdorf, and escorted by 4 Bf 109s of II. *Jagdgeschwader* 53 'Pik As' (transl. it. *Asso di picche*) by *Hauptmann* Gerhard Michalski stationed in Pantelleria. Having passed Cape Bon, some 18 miles northwest of the Isle of Dogs, the Italian-German airborne units appeared before the British convoy, which was sailing in four columns, at 18.36 hours and the spectacle the crews saw was impressive:

---

12 Set on the Tyne in 1913 as a battleship (as a liner according to the Marburger Zeitung of 12.08.1942) Chilean Almirante Cochrane was acquired by the Admiralty during the Great War and completed as an aircraft carrier in 1924 and refitted in 1932. During Operation *Pedestal*, the ship had a crew of 1,160 men, of whom 927 were rescued after torpedoing by the destroyers *HMS Laforey* and *HMS Lookout* and the tug *HM Jaunty*.

13 According to other sources, all 16 *Sea Hurricanes* embarked on the *HMS Eagle* went down with the ship.

14 The aircraft of the 132ⁿᵈ Autonomous Torpedo Group that took to the air at 17.30 on 12.08.1942 had the following military serial numbers (MM.): 23968, 24095 (torpedo not released due to failure of the release command), 24301, 24225, 24224, 24226, 24079, 24307, 24221, 22573, 24172, 24309, 24132 (MM. corresponding to FIAT B.R.20M, the correct number is likely to be 24312), 24313 (torpedo not released due to failure of release control). All the aircraft listed correspond to the SIAI S. 79S (torpedo version) except the one with MM. 22573 that corresponds to S. 79 or S. 79 bis (S.M. 84). The aircraft that did not release the torpedoes were piloted by Second Lieutenants Martino Aichner and Vittorio Moretti. Below are the MM numbers of the Whitehead (W) torpedoes dropped: 21300, 20272, 21284, 21247, 19286, 21269, 21268, 21272, 21280, 21265, 21266, 20261. Depth adjusted to 4 m. The other supplier was Silurificio Italiano (SI). The aeronautical torpedoes had a more disruptive explosive charge than the naval ones consisting of *Tritolital*. The W torpedo charge was 170 kg or 200 kg, the maximum diameter 450 mm, length 5.46 m and total weight 890 kg or 920 kg.

[...] in a great cloud of smoke (*it* is probable that the ships' crews used smoke bombs to reduce the convoy's visibility) the steamships and aircraft carriers stood in the centre and the warships surrounded them with a double circle of protection, at the top stood the umbrella of the hurricanes raised from the aircraft carriers (Bonvicini, Guido, Carlo Faggioni e gli aerosiluranti italiani, Milano, Cavallotti Editori, 1987).

'Torpedo bombers manoeuvred to attack from bow to starboard and from the side on the same side' (Fioravanzo, Giuseppe, *Le azioni navali in Mediterraneo, dal 1o aprile 1941 all 8 settembre 1943*, Roma, Ufficio Storico della Marina Militare, 1970). Soon the anti-aircraft guns arrived, exploding, marking the sky with dark clouds, and dense columns of black smoke began to rise from the sea covered in fuel slicks. The war mission was to:

[...] Attacking with torpedoes in the waters of the Isle of Dogs (off Tunisia) the most important merchantmen and warships of a powerful convoy coming from the west, composed of 21 steamers and escorted by two battleships, two aircraft carriers, six cruisers and 10 CC.TT. (destroyers *Ed*.), which once again attempted to force the Strait of Sicily with the intention of supplying the island of Malta (op. cit.).

The 'Sparrowhawks' of the 132nd Group[15] began the attack according to Rivoli's orders, dividing the formation 2 km from the convoy into extended patrols of 2-3 aircraft each, in order to better target the different targets. It was felt

[...] Faggioni's voice shouting into the laryngophone: «Give the buns!» It was almost his war cry repeated several times in jest even at the canteen or in the clubhouse (op. cit.).

Captain Graziani from Affile (Rome) and Lieutenant Vinciguerra from Catania went around two destroyers to attack a steamer. The patrol on the far left of the deployment, formed by 2 S. 79 of Lieutenant Carlo Faggioni from Carrara (LU), with the second pilot Winspeare from Naples to assist the first [the other crew members were: motor sergeant-major Ideale Facca from Azzano Decimo (Sacile), airman-at-arms Giovanni Capaldi from Cassino (FR), first airman-at-arms Italo Gianni from Venice and airman-at-arms photographer Loreto Daniello from Aversa (NA)] and his wingman, second lieutenant Martino Aichner from Trento, attacked another steamer, but the torpedo remained docked under the latter's aircraft due to the failure of the release mechanism[16]. On his return, Graziani reportedly asked Aichner for an explanation. Sub-Lieutenant Vittorio Moretti's torpedo from Genoa[17] also failed to disengage. Faggioni managed to disengage, followed by a violent turn to the right, at zero altitude, amidships and then zig-zagged between machine gun tracers and cannon blasts. Not all the torpedoes hit the mark either because they were not fired or because they were fired from too far away (600 to 900 m, 2,700 m according to Syfret's report) due to the extremely violent enemy anti-aircraft fire and the ships thus had time to evolve. On 12 August 1942, Second Lieutenant Carlo Winspeare took part in a

[...] torpedoing action against convoy of 21 steamers, escorted by 2 battleships, 2 aircraft carriers, several

---
15 Leading the crews of the attacking aircraft on 12 August 1942, were the following officers: Captain Ugo Rivoli, Lieutenant Francesco Bargagna, Lieutenant Guido Barani, Lieutenant Vittorio Moretti, Lieutenant Carlo Pfister, Lieutenant Mario Mazzocca, Lieutenant Giuseppe Coci, Captain Giulio Cesare Graziani, Lieutenant Carlo Faggioni, Lieutenant Marino Marini, Lieutenant Pasquale Vinciguerra, Lieutenant Martino Aichner, Lieutenant Paolo Manfredi, Lieutenant Aldo Migliaccio.
16 After the Battle of Mid-June, the sabotage of some torpedoes produced in the Silurificio di Baia (NA) was reported to the Military Court.
17 Initially, Sub-Lieutenant Moretti's crew was excluded from the transfer due to the unavailability of the equipment still being repaired. The officer protested and begged Commander Rivoli to let the repair crew work during the night. He was granted and was able to reach Pantelleria the following morning.

▲ *Bombs away!* Heavy bombs plummet on the Capodichino airfield on the outskirts of Naples in a raid by USAAF 'Flying Fortresses' (Boeing B-17s) from north-west Africa. At Capodichino, in November 1940, the 2nd Torpedo Training Unit was formed (photo taken from https://catalog.archives.gov/).

▲ Photo of 25-year-old second lieutenant A.A. r.n. pilot Carlo Winspeare taken on 23 April 1942 at the 2nd Aircraft Training Unit at Capodichino, Naples (photo g.c. Collection Edoardo Winspeare).

▼ The detail of the Winspeare coat of arms that once adorned Villa Salve on the Vomero hill seems reminiscent of the Order of Malta's insignia (author's photo).

cruisers and CC.TT., protected by unspecified Hurricanes. Torpedoed and sank 10,000-ton cruiser[18] under anti-aircraft reaction and enemy fighter attacks. Aircraft hit by shrapnel (Ministry of Defence, General Directorate for Military Personnel, III Department, Rewards and Honours Service, proposed Bronze Medal for Military Valour, Winspeare Carlo).

The 132nd Group was not disfigured thanks to the victory of Commander Rivoli who, at 18.43 hours, hit the stern, near the propellers, of the destroyer belonging to Force X *HMS Foresight* (*Lt Cdr* Robert Augustus Fell) of 1.428 t, causing irreparable damage, so she was sunk, near La Galite, northwest of Bizerte, by the similar *HMS Tartar* (*Capt* St. John Reginald Joseph Tyrwhitt), which had taken her in tow on a westerly course, at 09.55 the following day.

The mission had the following result:

[...] The torpedo planes plunged decisively into the intense anti-aircraft barrage and attacked the heavy cruiser and two large steamers in three formations. Three torpedoes were distinctly seen bursting against the heavy cruiser by all the specialists in the crews. Two steamers were also hit by one torpedo each. Enemy fighter aircraft of the Hurricane type, which attempted to attack the torpedo bombers, were promptly intercepted by the escorting Macchi 202s (op. cit.).

Thus, on the British side, *Vice Admiral* Edward Neville Syfret described the action:

[...] At 18.30 the first enemy formation was sighted... Against them we had 22 fighters in the air... The first attack began at 18:35 and included at least 13 torpedo bombers; at the same time an unknown number of high-altitude bombers, divers and minelayer planes attacked. An emergency turn was made to avoid the mines and torpedoes that had been dropped outside the starboard screen. After this, 40 torpedo bombers were reported, followed immediately by a Stuka attack against the INDOMITABLE, which was concealed by columns of water (generated by the bombs falling into the sea) and smoke. The end result of these series of hard attacks was the torpedoing aft of the FORESIGHT, the INDOMITABLE was hit by three (500 kg) large bombs... which caused two large fires and took out her flight deck (Syfret, Edward Neville, Operation «Pedestal», Supplement to The London Gazette of Tuesday, the 10th of August, 1948, London, His Majesty's Stationery Office, 1948).

The torpedo bomber formation, which had returned to Pantelleria (landing at 20.20), was attacked on the runway by *Beaufighters* coming from Malta between 21.10 and 22.03. An aircraft already parked caught fire and others were damaged by machine-gun fire, among them was 'Faà di Bruno'[19], Faggioni's aircraft. Second Lieutenant Pilot Moretti,

---

18 The only cruiser, which took part in Operation *Pedestal*, to have similar characteristics to those described was the ultra-modern *HMS Manchester* (*Capt* Harold Drew), with main armament 12 152 mm guns and a tonnage of 9,600 t (the light cruiser *HMS Cairo*, commanded by *Capt* Cecil Campbell Hardy, of 4.190 t was hit by the submarine Axum at about 20.00 hrs on 12.08.1942 and sank off Bizerte), although it was sunk by the Italian torpedo boats MS 16 (C.C. Giorgio Manuti) and MS 22 (S.T.V. Franco Mezzadra) at 01.07 hrs on 13 August 1942 near the Kelibia lighthouse (about 20 miles south of Cape Bon). The destroyer *HMS Pathfinder* embarked about 150 of her crew and later the remainder abandoned ship on *Carley floats* (life rafts *Ed.*). The 8,670-ton cruisers *HMS Nigeria* (*Capt* Stuart Henry Paton, flagship of the commander of the 10th Cruiser Squadron, *RAdm* Harold Martin Burrough) and the 8,720-ton *HMS Kenya* (*Capt* Alfred Spalding Russell) were torpedoed by the Italian submarines Axum (T.V. Renato Ferrini) at 20.00 hours and Alagi (T.V. Sergio Puccini) at 21.12 hours on 12 August 1942 respectively. It is possible that the three cruisers had been hit several times before, also by torpedo bombers, and that the results appreciated were much higher than the actual results (the same reasoning also applies to the other side).

19 In Faggioni's crew there was Airman Capaldi, who was a radio operator in the air and reported on the group's activities in some newspapers on the ground: [...] My aircraft was called 'Faà di Bruno' [...] Later there were those who found a significant correspondence between the two initials and the expression 'Faggioni di Buscaglia'; others saw in it a warning and, at the same time, a reminder of the unfortunate battle of Lissa. In reality, I invented that name and I no longer know

▲ Major Carlo Emanuele Buscaglia (22.09.1915-24.08.1944), was the commander of the 132nd Autonomous Torpedo Group. Believed dead in the Bougie roadstead after a torpedoing action, he was imprisoned in the Internment Camp in Crossville, Tennessee (USA). Returning home, he attempted to take off in a Baltimore bomber from Camp Vesuvius on 23 August 1944. Unfortunately, the plane lifted off the ground too early, touching the runway with its left wing, and caught fire. Buscaglia, burnt and injured, died the following day (photo taken from *Tempo*, op. cit. in bibliography).

[...] surprised by machine-gun fire from two enemy Beaufighter type aircraft, while on Pantelleria Airport he was rolling the aircraft to put it in the hangar, he was hit by machine-gun fire and died (op. cit.).

He ended up in the propeller blades of the right engine of his aircraft, which were still spinning. In addition to the above description of losses: 'Seven aircraft were hit in several places by the very violent reaction of the ships' (op. cit.). The observations concerning the day of 12 August were as follows:

[...] The crews gave a brilliant display of aggressiveness and fighting spirit, launching themselves into a formidable anti-aircraft fire in order to be able to release the torpedoes at short range... The action was combined with dive-bombing and our fighter escort. The tactical concept of the action, based on the massed use of aircraft against a limited number of units, was successful because it achieved concrete results.

Meanwhile, the convoy entered the waters of the Sicilian Channel via the Skerki Bank. For a good part of the navigation, thanks to the decryptions of *Ultra (Intelligence N.d.A.)*[20],

---

how it came to my mind. I think I included it in a war correspondence; Faggioni read that correspondence and liked the name. Faggioni read that correspondence and liked the name. He talked about it at length with me and ended up saying that he wanted that name on our aeroplane, and not on the nose, so that the others could read it, but on the nacelle, so that we could see it when we boarded it' (Bonvicini, Guido, *Carlo Faggioni e gli aerosiluranti italiani*, Milan, Cavallotti Editori, 1987).

20 The Regia Marina, starting in December 1940, adopted the Swedish cipher machine *C38m* (not to be confused with the more famous German *Enigma N.o.A.*) of Boris Hagelin (02.07.1892-07.09.1983) for message encryption. On 26.02.1941,

▲ A beautiful group photo in which the commander of the 132nd Autonomo Aerosiluranti Group, Carlo Emanuele Buscaglia, is standing in the centre; next to him, to his right, is a *Luftwaffe* officer. From the left, the first one crouching, holding his cap, is Carlo Winspeare (photo g.c. Collection Edoardo Winspeare).

▲ *Hurricane* aircraft shot down by Sicilian anti-aircraft defence on the night of 26 April 1942 at Gerbini, near Catania. The next morning Winspeare, who knew English perfectly, was sent by Buscaglia to check the papers of the pilot, a blond boy who seemed to be sleeping in the cockpit. 'The Germans have taken everything,' Aichner told him, 'all that's left is my identification card'; from the breast pocket of his jacket sprouted a yellow card on which was written: 'Sergeant Webster' (photo Istituto Luce, taken from: https://tecadigitaleacs.cultura.gov.it/).

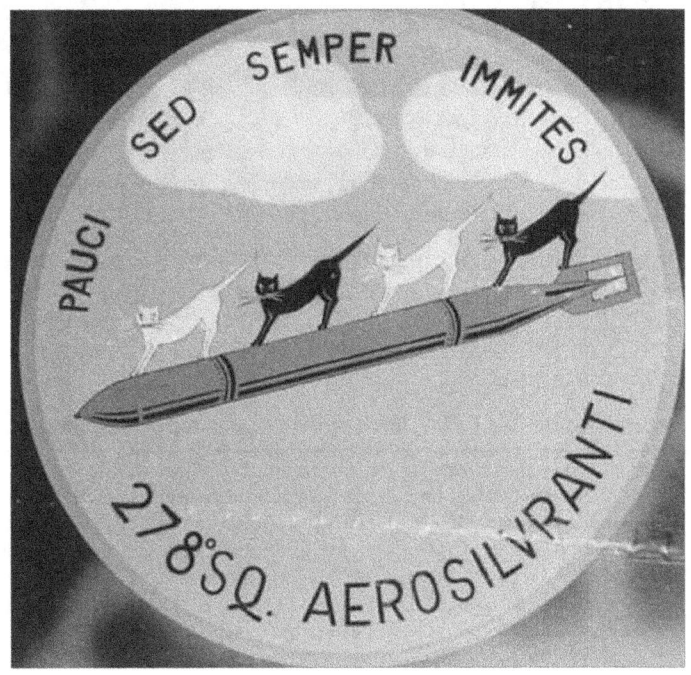

► The coat of arms adopted by the 278th Squadron (which together with the 281st Squadron formed the 132nd Torpedo Group) depicted 'the usual four cats' on a straight-tailed torpedo, two white (to bring good luck to the crews) and two black (to bring bad luck to the enemy), representing the initial number of aircraft in the unit's fleet. The motto *Pauci sed semper immites* meant 'Few but always impetuous' (photo Luciano Baldi via G. Maressi).

▲ German soldiers of the *Deutsches Afrikakorps* (DAK) on the deck of a ship anchored at the Naples Maritime Station in 1941. In the background you can make out the Maschio Angioino or Castel Nuovo, the Vomero hill with the Certosa di San Martino and, behind it, the Castel Sant'Elmo. The port of Naples was an important logistical hub for Axis convoys to and from Libya in North Africa (author photo).

the movements of the Italian cruisers were monitored. On the morning of Thursday 13 August,

[...] at 02.30 hrs, a squadron of the Regia Marina, consisting of 4 cruisers (the other 2 cruisers were damaged *Ed.*) and 8 destroyers, which was off the north-west coast of Sicily, returned (the 3ª Division with the Attendolo and the 7ª Division headed for Messina and Naples respectively) without making contact with the

during Operation *Abstention*, British *commandos* recovered the Y-1 cipher, the decryption book used by the Royal Ministry of Foreign Affairs, kept in the safe of the Governor's residence of Castelrosso in the Aegean Sea, the easternmost island of the Dodecanese. British *Ultra Intelligence* had its centre of operations on the Bletchley Park (BP) estate, where the *Government Code* and *Cipher School* (GC&CS) was relocated in the summer of 1940. The 'breaking' of the *C38m*, in the summer of 1941, by mathematician William Thomas Tutte (14.05.1917-02.05-2002), of BP's *Research Section* (later *Cryptographic Coordination and Record Section* or CCR), made it possible to decrypt thousands of intercepted radiomessages to the Regia Marina and, in large part, related to the traffic of supply convoys to North Africa. This was a turning point in the convoy battle in the Mediterranean.

▲ Carlo Winspeare posing on a fuel drum, wearing a white flight suit. Behind him, an S. 79, presumably in maintenance, appears to have its nose covered by a cloth. Under the wing can be seen the cockade with the three stylised lictor fasces (photo g.c. Collection Edoardo Winspeare).

▶ The emblem of the 132nd Autonomo Aerosilurant Group depicted the paladin Orlando, riding a winged horse armed with lance and shield, fighting a three-headed sea monster, on three lines was written the D'Annunzio motto: 'With heart and weapon beyond all goals' (author's photo).

▲ On the right, Carlo Winspeare smiling, in the 132nd Autonomous Torpedo Group's Headquarters hut, with other fellow soldiers. At his side hangs the 132nd Group's emblem (photo g.c. Collezione Edoardo Winspeare).

▼ The secretary of the Federazione dei Fasci di Combattimento di Catania, Antonio Mancia, visiting the Gerbini airfield, headquarters of the 132nd Autonomo Aerosiluranti Group. From left: Graziani, Rivoli, the federator, Winspeare, Buscaglia, Aichner, Bargagna, Pfister and Mazzocca. In the foreground Buscaglia (photo g.c. Collezione Edoardo Winspeare).

▲ Another image from the same series as the previous ones. In the foreground, Major Buscaglia, behind him on the right, Second Lieutenant Winspeare (photo g.c. Collection Edoardo Winspeare).

convoy (National Museum of the Royal Navy, Admiralty War Diaries, Mediterranean Fleet, July to September 1942, Mediterranean War Diary, August 1942).

The reason for this decision was probably due to the RAF's demonstration aimed at convincing the enemy that a much larger strike force was about to attack the Italian surface forces, which did not have an adequate air escort. Air actions resumed starting at 08.00 hours.

[...] Two S. 79 aircraft of the 278ª Squadron and one of the 281ª Squadron, returning from an attempted torpedo attack, landed with torpedoes on Castelvetrano Airport and remained there on alarm (op. cit.).

At 10.30 a.m. on a sweltering morning, the 132nd Group set off with the task of: 'to take the offensive again to the remains of the mighty convoy disrupted yesterday' (op. cit.) which were 130 km south-east of Pantelleria. So he sent a patrol of 5 of his torpedo bombers (3 aircraft of 278ª Squadron and 2 aircraft of 281ª Squadron), still under the orders of Rivoli[21], which included Faggioni [who had meanwhile passed on to another aircraft, taking with him the same crew as the previous day and the airman chosen photographer Ugo Vascellari from Calalzo (BL)], Graziani Lieutenant Guido Barani (from Comano, Apuania) and Second Lieutenant Carlo Pfister (from New York) with 14 fighter escorts of Major Fanali of the 155th Group, who managed to hit, but not sink, the refrigerated transport freighter *SS Port Chalmers* (*Capt* Henry George Bacon Pinkney, command ship of *Cdre* Albert George Venables) of 8.535 t:

---

[21] Leading the crews of the attacking aircraft on 13 August 1942 were the following officers: Captain Ugo Rivoli, Lieutenant Guido Barani, Second Lieutenant Carlo Pfister, Captain Giulio Cesare Graziani, Lieutenant Carlo Faggioni.

◄ Carlo Winspeare seated at the door of the barrack assigned to the 281ˢᵗ Sq. Aerosilurant (photo g.c. Collection Edoardo Winspeare).

► The runway of Gerbini Airport (CT): an aircraft attempts to take off to escape an Allied bombardment. In 1942, the command nucleus of the 132ⁿᵈ Autonomous Aero Group was based there under the command of Capt. (later Maj.) Carlo Emanuele Buscaglia with the 278ᵗʰ and 281ˢᵗ Squadrons (photo taken from https://catalog.archives.gov/).

[...] About 50 miles west of Malta seven steamers were sighted escorted by five cruisers and CC.TT. units and protected in flight by Spitfire type fighter aircraft. One large steamer was hit by torpedo. The effect of another torpedo, which the enemy attempted to sink with machine gunfire, was not observed, but given the testimony of the destroyer escort, it is believed that this torpedo also hit a large steamer (op. cit.).

On the other hand, this was the English version of the events just described:

[...] At 11.20 a.m. on 13 August 1942, Italian torpedo bombers carried out a combined attack with the launch of parachute mines or torpedoes with a spiral trajectory (i.e. the FFF motor bombs, named after their designers: Carlo Filpa, Amedeo Fiore and Prospero Freri, were a kind of torpedo falling into the water with a parachute, *ed.*) The torpedoes were launched from long range except for one that caught on the *SS Port Chalmers*' paramine (op. cit.).

The merchant ship's commander, seeing the dangerous circumstance, ordered the paramine cable to be cut and a strong pull to release the torpedo. In the action, Faggioni's aircraft was hit repeatedly. The torpedo bombers landed at 12.05 p.m., except for Barani's S. 79, which was riddled by the blasts of a *Spitfire* from 126 *Squadron*, plunging into the sea with its crew[22] : 'During the escape route, the formation of Aerosiluranti was attacked by Spitfire-type fighter aircraft, which shot down one of our aircraft in flames' (op. cit.). Barely half an hour after departure, the S. 79 of an emotional Rivoli returned for his fallen friend, followed by the other aircraft that had faced a more numerous and aggressive opponent.

22 [...] Crew of the downed aircraft: Lt. Pilot BARANI Guido, Sgt. M. (pilot *N.A.*) MAVILIO Fernando (from Pozzuoli, Naples), I° Av. Motor. FRANCO Italo (from Gorizia), I° Av. Marcon. PEDEMONTE Tullio (from Genoa), I° Av. Armiere TARTAGLIONE Giuseppe (from Marcianise, Caserta), Aviere All. Fotogr. FERRARI Vittorio (from Naples) (op. cit.).

▲ Vice Admiral Edward Neville Syfret (20.06.1886-10.12. 1972) in his office at the Admiralty in London; he was the commander of the convoy bound for Malta during Operation Pedestal after which he was made a Knight Commander of the Order of the Bath [...] For bravery and intrepid resolution in protecting with arms an important convoy to Malta in the face of relentless day and night attacks by enemy submarines, aircraft and surface forces (photo Ware, C. J., taken from https://commons.wikimedia.org/).

The British fighters were now more combative as defence for the convoy could be provided by the RAF directly from the nearby Malta base, which had been supplied with state-of-the-art aircraft in the previous days. On 13 August, in Malta waters, Winspeare took part in a

> [...] torpedoing action against convoy of 7 steamers escorted by 2 cruisers and 3 CC.TT. protected by 40 Spitfires. Torpedoed steamer[23] of 8,000 tons. Violent anti-aircraft reaction and repeated attacks by enemy fighters. 1 aircraft of the formation shot down and 1 hit by shrapnel (op. cit.).

The last task of the day (during most of which the planes could not take off due to the adverse weather conditions) of the 132nd Group, with the participation of 2 aircraft from 278^a Squadron and 1 aircraft from 281^a Squadron (led by the crews: Rivoli, Pfister, Graziani and Faggioni as the latter's second pilot) and departing at 19.05 hours, consisted of: "Search for and attack by torpedo a large enemy unit presumed to be damaged at the point of Lat. 37° 25' and Long. 9° 46" (op. cit.). But the result was not as hoped: 'The area between the 9th and 11th Meridians was thoroughly explored. The reported unit was not in said area' (op. cit.) . The units landed in Castelvetrano at 21.30[24] . In the evening, the vanguards of the *Pedestal*

---

[23] The other steamers to have similar characteristics to those described were: *SS Santa Elisa* (US, *Capt* Theodore Thompson) of 8,379 t hit by a Ju. 88, exploded at 05.30 hrs on 13 August 1942; *SS Deucalion* (*Capt* Ramsay Brown) of 7,516 t hit by He 111 at 21.30 on 12 August 1942, sank near the Isle of Dogs and survivors were recovered by the destroyer *HMS Bramham*; *SS Rochester Castle* (*Capt* Richard Wren) of 7,795 t hit by German aircraft at 20.35 on 12 August 1942 and torpedoed by Mas 564 (helmsman of 2^a class Giuseppe Iafrate) at 05.10 on 13 August 1942, after the German Ms *S 30* (*Lt zS* Horst Weber) had failed to hit her target at 03.14.

[24] For the sake of completeness, the following is what is written in the Historical Diary of the 132nd Aircraft Group for 14 and 15 August 1942 (op. cit.):

> [...] 14/8 <u>Variations in deployment</u> :
>
> The three aircraft that were at Castelvetrano Airport and five aircraft, two from 278^a Squadron and three from 281^a Squadron, which were at Pantelleria Airport, landed at Elmas Airport after performing a torpedoing action.
>
> <u>Efficient Luminaires</u> : S. 79 Silurant No.
>
> <u>War mission</u> :
>
> <u>Task</u> : Attack by torpedo an enemy naval formation consisting of a battleship, three cruisers and three CC.TT. sailing at Lat. 37° 18' and Long. 6° 22' on a westerly course.
>
> <u>Result</u>: The torpedo bomber aircraft, despite the intense and violent anti-aircraft fire of the units, attacked (at Cape Bougaroun N.A.) the battleship and a light cruiser in two formations. The 1st Airman Giannandrea, gunner of the last aircraft to make the attack, observed a column of water on the side of the light cruiser, which emitted another vertical column of smoke, as also observed by other crew members and documented by a photograph, and slowed his speed by pulling over.
>
> <u>Participating departments and equipment</u> :
>
> 278^a Squadron with 4 aircraft
>
> 281^a Squadron, with 4 aircraft.
>
> Departure 10.20 a.m. = Landing at Elmas 2.25 p.m.
>
> One aircraft was hit by anti-aircraft reactivity and returned to base with a laceration to the tailplane and another to the cockpit ceiling. One specialist was injured in the head by shrapnel from the anti-aircraft reaction.
>
> <u>Injured</u> :
>
> Av. Sc. Photographer CARINGELLA Giuseppe.
>
> These three successive torpedoing actions are to be considered among the riskiest and most brilliant to date. The proof given by the personnel who, with an unchanged aggressive and combative spirit, took part in these three successive attacks against the largest enemy convoy that has attempted to cross the Mediterranean should be noted.

convoy, escorted by minesweepers and motorboats, entered Malta's Grand Harbour. Italian aircraft carried out 11 main attacks on 12, 13 and 14 August 1942 ; on the other hand, German aircraft carried out 18 main attacks on 11, 12, 13 and 14 August 1942. Unfortunately, about 550 men perished during the battle: 450 (of whom 162 sank miserably with *HMS Eagle*) among the Allies and 100 (of whom 45 sank tragically with the RSmg Dagabur rammed by the destroyer *HMS Wolverine*) belonging to the Axis forces. The *Royal Navy*'s losses[25]

THE COMMANDER 132ND AUTONOMOUS GROUP. AEROSILURANTS

(Captain Pil. Carlo Emanuele BUSCAGLIA)

15/8 <u>Variations in deployment</u> :

The four aircraft of the 278ᵃ Squadron and the four aircraft of the 281ᵃ Squadron that were at Elmas Airport return to Gerbini. An S. 79 aircraft from the 2ⁿᵈ Aerosilurant Training Unit at Capodichino is assigned to the 278ᵃ Squadron.

<u>Efficient appliances</u> : S. 79 Siluranti No. 7

THE COMMANDER 132ND AUTONOMOUS GROUP. AEROSILURANTS

(Captain Pil. Carlo Emanuele BUSCAGLIA)

25   The Armed Forces Headquarters issued the following war bulletins:

Bulletin No. 804 of 10 August 1942:

[...] Day and night attacks were carried out by Axis aviation formations against Malta air bases (*Bulletin No. 804* in "il Resto del Carlino", year 58, No. 191, Bologna, Tuesday, 11 August, 1942).

Bulletin No. 805 of 11 August 1942:

[...] The bombing actions of the Axis Air Force continued against the Maltese airports: four 'Spitfires' were destroyed in air duels (*Bulletin No. 805* in 'il Resto del Carlino', year 58, No. 192, Bologna, Wednesday, 12 August, 1942).

And Bulletin No. 806 of 12 August 1942:

[...] British air raids on Catania and various places in the Province of Cagliari caused two dead and three wounded. In the western Mediterranean, at dawn yesterday, one of our submarines attacked a large warship of an unspecified type that was heavily escorted, hitting it with two torpedoes (*Bulletin No. 806* in "Cronache della Guerra", Rome, Year IV, No. 34, 22 August 1942).

Followed by Bulletin No. 807 of 13 August 1942:

[...] In the western Mediterranean, a large enemy convoy, escorted by an impressive number of warships, including several aircraft carriers, was sighted from dawn on the 11ᵗʰ and attacked by powerful airborne formations and Axis submarines. The action, which is still in progress, has already yielded results favourable to us: heavy losses were inflicted on the convoy, the escort ships, particularly the aircraft carriers that were suffering the hardest blows, and the enemy's airborne formations. These losses will be detailed later (*Bulletin No 807* in 'La Battaglia del Canale di Sicilia, Mezz'agosto 1942-XX', Rome, Istituto Romano di Arti Grafiche, 1942).

Followed by Extraordinary Bulletin No. 808 (also issued on 13 August 1942):

[...] At dawn on 11 August, in the western Mediterranean, our submarines and reconnaissance planes sighted a large enemy convoy of more than 20 steamers sailing from Gibraltar to the east, escorted by three battleships, four aircraft carriers, numerous cruisers, several dozen destroyers and smaller units. From the morning of the 11ᵗʰ, the action of the closely co-operating Italian and German air and naval forces began against the important enemy formation. Our submarines, Mas and torpedo bombers, squadrons of high-altitude and dive bombers and torpedo bombers with large numbers of fighters, acting en masse, took turns in the attack, torpedoing and bombarding numerous units of the convoy, despite the extremely violent anti-aircraft fire and the reaction of the enemy fighters. Overall, the following losses were inflicted on the enemy:

by the Regia Marina: 1 cruiser and 3 steamers sunk;

by R. Aeronautica vehicles: 1 cruiser, 1 destroyer and 3 steamers sank;

by German naval aircraft: in addition to the sinking of the aircraft carrier 'Eagle', four steamships were sunk.

Numerous other merchantmen and warships, including one battleship and two aircraft carriers (one of which *was* the 22,500-ton *HMS Furious*), were hit, some several times and so severely that their subsequent sinking was highly pro-

were (number of casualties in brackets): 1 aircraft carrier [*HMS Eagle* (162)], 2 cruisers [*HMS Cairo* (23) and *HMS Manchester* (11)] and 1 destroyer [*HMS Foresight* (5)] sunk; 1 aircraft carrier [*HMS Indomitable* (52)], 2 cruisers [*HMS Kenya* (4) and *HMS Nigeria* (50)] and 2 destroyers (*HMS Wolverine* and *HMS Ithuriel*) damaged. To these were added the 6 casualties of *HMS Victorious* and the losses of the British merchant navy: 9 steamers sunk [*MV Empire Hope, SS Dorset, MV Wairangi, MV Waimarama* (73), *SS Almeria Lykes* (US), *SS Santa Elisa* (US), *SS Clan Ferguson* (11), *MV Glenorchy* (7), *SS Deucalion*]; 2 steamers [*MV Brisbane Star* (1) and *SS Rochester Castle*] and 1 tanker (*SS Ohio*) damaged. Although she managed to land in Malta, the *MV Melbourne Star* counted 9 casualties. While Regia Marina's losses were: 2 submarines [RSmg Dagabur (45) and RSmg Cobalt (2)] sunk; 2 cruisers [RN Bolzano (9) and RN Attendolo] and 1 submarine [RSmg Giada (1)] damaged. In contrast, the *Kriegsmarine* lost the motor torpedo boat S 58. Losses among British aircraft belonging to the *Fleet Air Arm* (FAA) and RAF Malta amounted to 36 aircraft. On the other hand, Regia Aeronautica losses amounted to 42 aircraft. The *Luftwaffe* lost 19 aircraft among which there were at least 15 Ju. 88, 1 Ju. 87 and 1 Bf 109 shot down with 9 confirmed dead, 51 missing (of which 11 rescued or returned) and 3 wounded[26]. Despite the fact

bable. In extremely hard fighting engaged by our hunters, who dominated the skies of the battle, 32 enemy aircraft were shot down; 13 of our aircraft did not return to base, many others returned with dead and wounded on board. The most important part of the escort convoy made its way back, under the uninterrupted action of our aircraft. A fraction of the convoy tried to reach Malta pursued and hammered by German and Italian aviation (*Extraordinary Bulletin No. 808* in "Il Piccolo", Trieste, Friday 14 August 1942).

To which was added Bulletin No. 809 of 14 August 1942:

[...] In the Mediterranean, in further actions against the surviving portions of the enemy convoy attacked in the previous days, new successes were achieved. Submarines and small torpedo boat units sank a cruiser, a destroyer and 3 merchant ships; torpedo bombers and torpedo bombers sank 4 steamers and hit a battleship sailing towards Gibraltar with two torpedoes; German naval units sank 4 merchant ships. The aircraft carrier hit on the 11th by the submarine Uarsciek and returned damaged to Gibraltar was the Furious. Among the cruisers sunk by us is the ultra-modern Manchester. Many enemy shipwrecks were picked up and concentrated in our naval bases or hospitals. Others flocked to the Tunisian coast. A further 10 enemy aircraft were shot down by Italian-German fighters; our losses rose to 19 aircraft. Two of our units of the R. Marina, of medium tonnage, were damaged and one of them seriously (*Bulletin No. 809* in "Stampa Sera", year 76, No. 194, Turin, Friday, 14-15 August, 1942).

And Bulletin No. 810 of 15 August 1942:

[...] Yesterday, our air and naval forces continued their action against the dispersed warship nuclei that had already escorted the enemy convoy, constantly monitored by our aerial reconnaissance, which had been working tirelessly since the beginning of the battle. A mas torpedoed a destroyer from a short distance; dive formations hit a large-tonnage ship with large-calibre bombs; a torpedo bomber patrol hit a heavy cruiser; another torpedo bomber formation hit a cruiser and put a torpedo on the bow of a battleship. Our destroyer escorts shot down four Spitfires. Some crews of aircraft lost in the previous days were rescued by rescue seaplanes… Over Valletta harbour and Micabba airfield, Axis aviators dropped bombs of various calibres; one enemy aircraft was shot down. From the day's war missions, 6 of our aeroplanes did not return (*Bulletin No. 810* in "il Resto del Carlino", year 58, No. 195, Bologna, Monday, 17 August, 1942).

Instead, the following is the English Radio Bulletin of 19.08.1942:

[...] In it it is announced that, in addition to the Pa *Eagle* and Inc *Manchester*, the Inc c.a. were also sunk. *Cairo* and the Ct *Foresight*. The total number of aircraft destroyed in the battle amounted to 66, while the losses in aircraft on the British side amounted to 8 aircraft, while 4 pilots of these were rescued… The *Foresight* was torpedoed by an aircraft and towed for 12 hours; but later it too had to be sunk by British ships (op. cit.).

26 Here are the rank; the pilot's first name and surname; the department; the model, identification and serial number of the aircraft; and the date the aircraft was shot down during the *Pedestal* and *Bellows* operations from 10 to 14 August 1942: *Fw* Walter Bastian, 1/LG-1, Ju. 88A-4, L1 + EH, 140074, 12.08.1942; *Uffz* Gerhard Böhr, 3/LG-1, Ju. 88A-4, L1 + BL, 5551, 13.08.1942; *Obfw* Helmut Deidlauf, 5/LG-1, Ju. 88A-4, L1 + GN, 140101, 12.08.1942; *Obfw* Siegfried Fiedler, 6/LG-1, Ju. 88A-4, L1 + AP, 140197, 12.08.1942.1942; *Oblt* Helmut Axel Gerlich, 5/LG-1, Ju. 88A-4, L1 + ON, 142203, 12.08.1942; *Uffz* Herbert Gössling, I/StG-3, Ju. 87D-3, CG + SA or CG + SK, 2711, 13.08.1942; *Lt* Hans-Ernst Hamann, 6/LG-1, Ju. 88A-4,

that 64.3 per cent of the *W.S.21S.* convoy had been sunk and 21.4 per cent damaged, five surviving ships managed to arrive in Malta with 32,000 t of vital supplies for the starving island, which were unloaded by 22 August 1942 by soldiers of the Malta garrison. This task was called Operation *Ceres*[27]. Malta thus continued to be a thorn in the side for the Axis forces in the Mediterranean theatre. According to the Anglo-American press, a total of 66 (probably 100 counting damaged) Axis aircraft were destroyed and the RAF lost 8 aircraft. *Vice Admiral* Syfret wrote in his report on Operation *Pedestal*: 'The fact that 39 aircraft were definitely shot down by them and the probability that at least as many were rendered unserviceable is an exceptional measure of the success of the aircraft carriers' (op. cit.). Also in the same report, Syfret described that among the enemy aircraft: 26 had been shot down (including 3 Ju. 88s and 2 Ju. 87s), 9 were probably shot down (including 4 Ju. 88s, 1 Ju. 87, 1 torpedo bomber and 1 minelayer) 1 (*Stuka* or "Picchiatello") presumed shot down and 5 damaged (including 2 Ju. 88s). While, on the British side, 6 aircraft were shot down (including 1 *Spitfire*, 1 *Hurricane* and 1 *Fulmar*) and 1 aircraft forced to land; 2 pilots were rescued and the crews of 2 aircraft were recovered. For Air Squadron General Giuseppe Santoro, during the Battle of Mid-August, 19 Regia Aeronautica aircraft were shot down (including 6 S. 79, 6 Ju. 87, 5 Re. 2001 and 2 S. 84), 1 S. 79 landed in Tunisia and 63[28] crewmen fell, in addition to the 2 killed in the machine-gun attack on the airports of Elmas and Decimomannu (and Second Lieutenant Vittorio Moretti *N.d.A.*). The bulletins of the Armed Forces Headquarters report (see also footnote 21), however, that 47 enemy aircraft were shot down and 25 of our aircraft did not return. The newspapers of the time extolled the feat of the Regia Aeronautica and Regia Marina troops with headlines such as the following: "The aircraft carrier 'Eagle' sunk" (Corriere della Sera, Wednesday, 12 August 1942), "Powerful attack on a convoy escorted by an impressive fleet" (Le Ultime Notizie, Il Piccolo at eighteen o'clock, Thursday, 13 August 1942), "British convoy decimated" (Il Piccolo, Friday, 14 August 1942), "Three warships and ten steamers sunk" (Il Resto del Carlino, Friday 14th August 1942), "The annihilation of the enemy convoy" (Il Mattino, Saturday 15th August 1942), "No transport escaped the massacre" (La Stampa, Saturday 15th August 1942), "Ships on fire off the Tunisian coast" (Il Messaggero, Saturday 15th August 1942); and even the Duce issued a proclamation of praise addressed to the

> [...] Officers, non-commissioned officers, graduates, sailors and airmen! On 11, 12, 13 August you have, after a bitter battle, annihilated the enemy naval forces that had once again attempted to venture on the sea of Rome. The enemy, usually so reticent and tardy, was forced, given the severity of his catastrophe, to confess his losses and acknowledge your shining victory. Crashed by your bombs and torpedoes, its ships lie at the

---

L1 + HP, 140090, 12.08.1942; *Uffz* Franz Hronek, 2(F)/122, Ju. 88A-4, F6 + FK, 2174, 11.08.1942; *Oblt* Leopold Lagauer, 8/KG-77, Ju. 88A-4, 3Z + ES, 2158, 12.08.1942.1942; *Fw* Hugo Langer, 2/JG-77, Bf 109F-4, 13190, 13.08.1942; *Obfw* Heinz Limmertz, 4/KG-77, Ju. 88A-4, 3Z + FM, 142177, 14.08.1942; *Hptm* Werner Lüben, Stfkpt 2/LG-1, Ju. 88A-4, L1 + YK, 140105, 12.08.08.1942; *Lt* Karl-Erich Ritter, 1/KGr-806, Ju. 88A-4, M7 + DH, 140701, 11.08.1942; *Uffz* Hans Schmiedgen, 2(F)/122, Ju. 88D-1, F6 + KK, 430274, 13.08.1942; *Lt* Leo Skrdla, 3/KGr-806, Ju. 88A-4, M7 + GL, 8619, 11.08.1942; *Hptm* Werner Tronicke, 3/KGr-806, Ju. 88A-4, M7 + DL, 5829, 12.08.1942; *Fw* Werner Vogt, 1/LG-1, Ju. 88A-4, L1 + OH, 5600, 12.08.1942.

27 Ceres, in Latin *Ceres, Cereris*, was the Italic goddess of the harvest and fertility of the fields; in iconography she was depicted with a crown of ears of corn on her head while holding a bunch of ears of corn in her hand.

28 This figure has been extrapolated by multiplying the number of downed aircraft, described in the work of Giuseppe Santoro (Naples, 09.11.1894-02.06.1975) sub-chief of staff of the Regia Aeronautica during the Second World War, by the number of members of their respective crews, so it is only an estimate. Fortunately, a downed aircraft was not always matched by the loss of its crew. For example, cases of recovery by hydro-rescue are known. Probably, a large proportion of the crew members were saved.

bottom of the Mediterranean. The German comrades, in fraternal emulation with you, fought day and night by your side and inflicted deadly blows on the enemy. Officers, non-commissioned officers, graduates, sailors and airmen! In the short cycle of two months, you have bent the pride of that which was once the ruler of the seas to the point of bitter humiliation, you have diminished its prestige and power. The Italian people is proud of you, I salute the King! MUSSOLINI (Proclamation of the Duce to the Navy and Air Force, Armed Forces Headquarters, 15 August 1942).

On the German side, on the other hand, communiqués were issued by the Supreme Command of the Armed Forces (transl. ted. *Oberkommando der Wehrmacht*) in which the German-Italian collaboration was emphasised:

[...] This convoy... in spite of very strong anti-aircraft and air defences has been attacked in the western Mediterranean since 11 August in continuous, extensive and exemplary cooperation of the German and Italian Allied air and sea forces (Germanic Extraordinary Communiqué, Führer Headquarters, 13 August 1942).

[...] The victorious combat is a page of glory of the cooperation between the Allied forces of water and air and of the exemplary valour of all the soldiers who took part in it in the air and on board the warships (Extraordinary communiqué, Führer's Headquarters, 15 August 1942).

The commander of 281ª Squadron, Captain Giulio Cesare Graziani, wrote in his report, attached to the proposal sheet for the Bronze Medal for Military Valour (MBVM), that Winspeare had taken 'two successive torpedoing actions' and that he was on board 'the

▲ The aircraft carrier HMS Eagle (94), on 11 August 1942 was sunk by the German submarine U-73 commanded by kapitänleutnant Helmut Rosenbaum, as seen from the flight deck of the aircraft carrier HMS Indomitable where Fairey Albacore and Hawker Hurricane aircraft are stationed, during a convoy bound for Malta (photo Roper, F. G., taken from https://commons.wikimedia.org/).

▲ The Straits of Sicily (Strasse von Sizilien), German airborne forces were also employed in the Battle of Mid-August (photo taken from Der Adler, op. cit. in bibliography).

same aircraft S.M. 79 as Faggioni', as second pilot. The Commander of the 132nd Autonomo Aerosiluranti Group, Major Buscaglia, and the Commander of the Sicilian Air Force, General Scaroni, were of the same opinion. Thus Second Lieutenant Winspeare was decorated with the Bronze Military Valour Medal 'in the field' for having taken part in the Battle of Mid-August, here is the motivation:

[...] A torpedo aircraft pilot took part in two successive attacks against an enemy convoy escorted by warships. Heedless of the violent anti-aircraft reaction and the repeated attacks of the enemy fighter, he dropped torpedoes at a short distance from the targets, contributing to sinking a heavy cruiser and damaging other warships and merchant vessels. Mediterranean Sky 12-13 August 1942 - XX (1943 concession).

The other members of his crew were awarded a Silver Medal for Military Valour and five Military Crosses.

Again the grandson, Edoardo, tells us:

[...] I also believe that ... after an initial period of warlike enthusiasm, the uncle had suffered a very strong shock; I do not know if it was on a specific occasion or because he had opened his eyes to the true face of war. The fact is that, from a certain moment on, he decided that he would never again kill a human being. To be true to this vow, when he was on a mission over the Mediterranean, he would fire his torpedoes into the sea before reaching the enemy target. It's a beautiful story, albeit an incredible one... I imagine that facing death every day sent him into a deep crisis that must have haunted him until the end of his life... I know for sure that he refused to drop bombs on Valletta - which, not coincidentally, was the city where he was born - and perhaps this was the trigger for his conversion to pacifism (op. cit.).

After this feat, 'ours' was a day officer in the group for 5 and 23 August 1942. In addition, he was entrusted with the job of ordinary material warehouse officer. He did not shine in this last task, perhaps because it deprived him of the reckless ventures that could be made in the sky and because of his excesses of generosity: "[...] at every end-of-month inventory he was obliged to make up, with his own money, the lack of shirts and *footwear* that were regularly missing from the roll-call...". (Aichner, Martino, Il Gruppo Buscaglia, Aerosiluranti italiani nella seconda guerra mondiale, Milan, Mursia, 1991). On 8 September 1942, at Airport No. 505 (Gerbini), second lieutenant pilot Carlo Winspeare, of the 281ª Squadron Aerosiluranti, declared (or had to declare in order to continue serving in the Regia Aeronautica *N.d.A.*) that he did not belong to the Jewish race[29], including his parents; that he was not a member of the Israelite community; that he did not profess the Jewish religion; that he professed the Roman Apostolic Catholic religion; that he had not converted to another religion and had never been a member of the associations contemplated by Law No. 2029[30]. In early October, the 132ⁿᵈ Autonomous Aerosilurant Group moved from Gerbini to Pantelleria for an operational stop. Pilot Captain Giulio Cesare Graziani, Commander of the 281ª Aerosiluranti Squadron, wrote the following information report on him, dated 29 December 1942, at Trapani-Chinisia Airport No. 516 (PM 3550) where the 132ⁿᵈ Group was transferred to in mid-December for the Anglo-American landings in Morocco and Algeria:

[...] From 25/4/1942 to 23/12/1942 I had in my employ S. Lt. Compl. WINSPEARE Carlo, of healthy constitution but excessively puny. Frequents sports in general and can swim very well. Of frank, good and loyal character, generous and sensitive soul. Very courteous and gentlemanly with colleagues, respectful with superiors with little or no authority with inferiors. His personality as an officer can be said to be unformed. His general education was excellent, but his technical and professional education was good. Officer in charge of the Office of Ordinary Material, he did not carry out his duties with sufficient diligence and parsimony, causing the Department to incur two conspicuous charges. Wore the uniform with decorum. Still inexperienced young pilot, but full of enthusiasm. Volunteered for the specialty of Aerosilurant where, due to insufficient training, he was unable to perform actions as a crew chief. During the Battle of Mid-August, he took part in

---

29 The Fascist racial laws were in force. They were a series of legislative and administrative measures, approved in Italy between the end of 1938 and the first half of the 1940s, mainly directed against the Jews and first announced by Benito Mussolini on 18.09.1938 in Trieste. While these measures were repealed in the Kingdom of the South at the beginning of 1944, they continued to remain in force in the territory of the RSI until April 1945.

30 This is Law No. 2029 of 26.11.1925 on the regularisation of the activities of Associations, Bodies and Institutes and the membership thereof of personnel employed by the State, Provinces, Municipalities and Institutes subject by law to the protection of the State, Provinces and Municipalities.

two risky actions, cooperating very well with the Crew Chief. He was awarded a V.M. Bronze Medal. As crew chief, he carried out long reconnaissance missions in the open sea with night-time returns (op. cit.).

Because of the episode described by Graziani, Carlo Winspeare was given a punishment: "[...] on the occasion of the transfer of the Department to another Base, he did not take care with due discipline of the deposit of the items of equipment taken, causing harmful dispersions". During his military career, he accumulated 6 punishments (for disobedience, expulsion and disciplinary violation *N.d.A.*) all pardoned on the occasion of the 20th anniversary of the March on Rome or cancelled for five years[31] . Withheld from military service by authority for exceptional military needs from 29 October 1942, on 10 December 1942 he was admitted to the military hospital in Palermo due to illness, thus ceasing to be mobilised and to be in the area of operations, although he remained in territory declared to be in a state of war. It was probably on this occasion that he contracted a venereal disease that made him sterile. On 19 December 1942, he was discharged from the aforementioned hospital and sent on a 30-day convalescence leave, thus ceasing to be in declared state-of-war territory. During this period he was assigned to the 14th Group "C" (Complementary) based in Reggio Emilia on 23 December 1942. He returned from the aforementioned leave on 19 January 1943, thus finding himself once again in territory declared in a state of war and zone of operations, having been mobilised. On 20 April 1943, he was authorised to wear the 1st grade badge (bronze) of the specialty Aerosiluranti by the Air Force Command of Sicily. From 24 February 1943, he was assigned to the 10th Terrestrial Bombardment Wing, 32nd Group, 57a Squadron, based at Jesi (AN) airfield No. 265 (PM 3200) as a flight office officer, while from 15 July 1943 he attended the Scuola di Volo Senza Visibilità (SVSV) in Cameri[32] in the province of Novara.

[...] When the armistice was announced by radio Algiers, the Regia Aeronautica divisions were left to fend for themselves: no orders had been issued in advance. In the Supreme Command's Memo No. 1, sent to the three General Staffs on 4 September 1943, the following was written for the Aeronautica: a) The fighter divisions must be concentrated in the Lazio airports, the remaining specialities in Sardinia and any aircraft

---

31 Below are the dates, the authorities who inflicted them, the species, duration and reasons for the punishments:

13/11/41 Com. Aerop. - Capodichino A.S. (simple arrests *N.d.A.*) - gg. 5 - "As a flight officer he did not take timely care of the airfield razing, after an enemy bombing action". CONDONED on the occasion of the 20th anniversary of the March on Rome (D. M. 39750 of 16-11-1942 XXI)

23/1/42 " " - " A.R. (rigorous arrests *N.d.A.*) - gg. 5 - "Officer on flights from 2 p.m. to 3 p.m. made himself unavailable and then left the service before the deadline". CONDONED on the occasion of the 20th anniversary of the March on Rome (D. M. 39750 of 16-11-1942 XXI)

15/3/42 " " - " A.S. - gg. 5 - "Flight officer left the airport for about 2 hours without authorisation from the competent superior". CONDONED on the occasion of the 20th anniversary of the March on Rome (D. M. 39750 of 16-11-1942 XXI)

9/10/42 Comm. 132nd Aut. Aerosil. - A.S. gg 3 - "Officer in charge of Ordinary Material, on the occasion of the transfer of the Department to another Base, did not take care with due discipline of the pouring of the items of equipment taken, causing harmful dispersions". CONDONED on the occasion of the 20th anniversary of the March on Rome (Ministerial Decree 39750 of 16-11-1942 XXI)

15/4/1943 Com. 10th Wing - A.S. gg. 5 - "In training flight he did not follow the rules given by the Squadron Commander". CANCELLED FOR FIVE YEARS' COMPLETION (*Art. 26 of Ord. 3 ed. 1930-Reprint 1943*)

20/4/43 From C.S. - A.S. days 3 - "Flight duty commander showed up 10 minutes late". CANCELLED FOR COMPLETION OF FIFTEEN YEARS (*Art. 26 of Ord. 3 ed. 1930-Reprint 1943*).

32 Before that date, the Unvisited Flying School was located in Littoria where the 132nd Group was also located, and was later transferred to Cemeri (NO). At the same time, another SVSV operated at Linate (MI).

▲ The iconic single-engine, low-wing *Supermarine Spitfire* fighter, probably a photographic reconnaissance model, flies over the Pigeon Rocks near Beirut in Lebanon in 1942. The aircraft was friendly called 'Spit' by the British. It not infrequently happened that, aircraft normally based in the Middle East, operated from Malta to take the offensive over Bel Paese territory (photo Spurr Algy, g.c. Collection Brian Spurr).

▼ "Everything and everybody for victory", 50 cent stamp of the imperial series issued on 12 August 1942. On the war propaganda appendix, dedicated to the Regia Aeronautica, are imprinted the S. 79 aircraft that Lindbergh called "the best bombers in the world" (author's photo).

not in condition to take off must be destroyed... Only the Regia Aeronautica General Staff was aware of these orders; no orders of any kind reached the periphery (Pesce, Giuseppe, L'Aeronautica Italiana nella guerra di Liberazione).

The day after 8 September, 'ours' found shelter at Villa Boccabianca[33] in Cupra Marittima (AP) owned by the Vinci family, his friends. In the diaries of 'Babka', i.e. Countess Andreola Vinci Gigliucci[34], there is a trace of his stay:

[...] on 14 September the first two Allied prisoners to be hidden signed the book leaving their addresses: Clifford Irvine and Williams Evans. Then it was the turn of Carlo Winspeare, Uguccione (Ranieri Bourbon del Monte, complementary artillery lieutenant, *editor's note*), Dino Philipson (complementary artillery major, *editor's* note) and Roberto Bondi (civilian, class of 1907)... Friday 17 September [...] This afternoon, drenched in sweat and breathless, Carlo Winspeare arrived on a bicycle (which would later be taken by the Germans, *editor's note).*) Carlo Winspeare, escaped from the Jesi airfield (he crossed the lines determined to fulfil his oath of allegiance to the king, at the risk of being deported to Germany *Ed.*), occupied by the Germans along with Ancona... Philipson and Carlo Winspeare would like to rent a boat to go south because, between the main road full of Germans and the Militia, which seems to be running trains again, it is not safe to travel by land. Saturday 18 September [...] Carlo Winspeare has rheumatic pains and a fever... Tuesday 21 September [...] Carlo Winspeare is in bed with colitis... Monday 4 October [...] poor Carlo Winspeare, ever thinner and paler, busy with a continuous up and down at the W.C. because of his interminable colitis, is the *souffre-douleur* (laughing stock) of everyone. Papa (Giorgio Vicino Pallavicino, Reserve Cavalry Colonel, Army Staff, *editor's note*) scolds him, or rather shouts at him for being distracted and dragging his feet, Uguccione harasses him and practices on him to learn how to give injections, Philipson teases him saying that women have ruined him. Tuesday 5 October [...] The motorman Pizza came in the afternoon to say that the motorboats had been ordered by the Germans to turn themselves in at Ancona and that, in order to save their boats, the ship-owners had all put out to sea during the night yesterday. Only one remained that would leave at dusk and it had to be taken advantage of immediately. Great confusion in the house for the departure preparations. [...] Carlo Winspeare was losing everything, including his head, for which I gave him a hood of mine that made him look more like an elf than ever. Wednesday 6 October [...] The boat is big, one of those they use for the coastguard, but they haven't found the sailors and the fuel is not enough. Uguccione and Carlo Winspeare have remained to guard the boat and hope to have everything ready by tomorrow. Thursday 7 October [...] Today it poured all day... Dad, disgusted, wants nothing more to do with the expedition and Roberto Bondi, very sceptical, has also stayed at home. Only Philipson went to San Benedetto in the evening to see what became of the boat. He returned in high spirits. He found Uguccione and Carlo Winspeare in a pitiful state: they had spent a hellish night on hard bedding, in the dark, puking their souls out inside the boat, which was jumping over the waves at the mouth of the harbour. After dinner he came to the room and made me laugh a lot describing the destroyed faces of those two. It seems that tomorrow there will be the sailors, the rest of the oil and everything needed for departure. Friday 8 October [...] At 4.30 a.m. Dad, Philipson and Roberto Bondi were getting ready to leave when Nino Pettenello and a friend, a certain Gianni da Campo, who had escaped from Venice, where university students are forced to serve in the militia (the Guardia Nazionale Repubblicana or GNR *Ed.*), appeared. They too are on their way to Badoglian troops. We proposed that they leave immediately with the others, but Philipson didn't seem at all enthusiastic about joining the expedition with those two youngsters... 2 November [...] Uguccione told me about his journey with his father and his comrades: the compass didn't

---

33 One of the main bases of the 'Ratberry Line' or 'Rat-Line' (not to be confused with the *Rattenlinien*, i.e. the escape routes followed by Nazis and collaborationists in the post-war period to go, mainly, to South America *Ed.*), used to free former prisoners of war such as those who were held in the Prisoners of War Camp 59 (PG59) in Servigliano (FM).
34 Andreola, born Vicino Pallavicino, married Count Zeno Vinci Gigliucci, was a cultured artist and kept a diary in which she noted down the main events in and around Boccabianca. The couple, both anti-fascists and Anglophiles, spent the war years on the Boccabianca property where they gave refuge to escaped prisoners of war (POWs). They were also forced to house German and fascist contingents on the same property.

work, the fuel was low and by sheer miracle they managed to enter the port of Tremiti slowly, where they met an English ship. Refuelled with oil, Philipson, Roberto Bondi and Carlo Winspeare continued on to Bari while Dad and Uguccione embarked with the British. They disembarked in Termoli... (Perini, Alessandro, I diari di Babka, 1943-1944 antifascist aristocracy and secret missions, Lulu.com, 2007).

Traces of this kind of action can also be found in the British Archives:

[...] 4. Nov. A boat carrying five former prisoners of war arrived in Termoli from San Benedetto. This 'coup d'état' had been successfully organised by Agent FAUSTO[35], of this Section, who had originally landed on 22 October, one of the six Agents who were working as a team (see Plan RATBERRY Section "A"). (IS9[36] Progress Report from 4 to 21 November 1943).

For taking part in this action, Carlo Winspeare, was decorated for the second time with the Bronze Medal for Military Valour (this time awarded by the Army as it was an event related to the resistance *N.d.A.*) with the following motivation:

[...] Surprised by the events of 8 September 1943 in German-occupied territory, he was determined to put his activity at the service of his homeland and, with four other brave men, managed to take possession of a patrol boat in the service of the enemy, sail out of S. Benedetto del Tronto at night and reach the liberated territory of Manfredonia at dawn. The twelve-hour crossing was left to fate because they were without any seafaring experience, equipped with only a makeshift compass and with a limited amount of fuel. The boat taken from the Germans was then handed over to the Italian Navy. Adriatic Sea 8-9 September 1943 (*Ministry of Defence - Army - Official Bulletin - Dispensa 7ª - Year 1949 - Rewards*, p. 1294).

The other four 'Argonauts' who, together with him, took part in the crossing on board the patrol boat, were also rewarded with the Bronze Medal for Military Valour. But how did the Aerosiluranti feel in the aftermath of the armistice? The following words explain it quite well:

[...] Many, following their instinct, which had always been an instinct of rebellion, went to the North. But even those who went to the South brought with them the same style of rebellion. The drama of the armistice was felt above all in the south. The legal airmen did not hide their envy when they learnt that the 'northerners' (like Carlo Faggioni *N.d.A.*), the illegals, the rebels, could still fight with the "hunchbacks" full of glory and aches and pains, and continued to be aerosilurers while they, with the damned Baltimore... were entrusted with marginal and unwelcome tasks, such as transport or bombing in distant areas, in Yugoslavia for example, in support of the armed bands of a leader like Tito, whom many still insisted on considering a sworn enemy of the Italians. (Chiocci, Francobaldo, Gli Affondatori del Cielo, Rome, Ed. Il Borghese, 1972).

After 8 September, part of the 132nd Aerosilurant Group (another part of the personnel

---

35 Fausto Simonetti, born on 20 February 1921 in Palmiano di Venarotta (AP), student of medicine and surgery. A Regia Aeronautica soldier, possibly in the Medical Corps, he was commander of a partisan formation (he belonged to the Banda S. Marco from 13.09.1943 to 05.10.1943 and to the Banda Stipa from 06.10.1943 to 06.06.1944) during the fighting at Colle San Marco. Brought numerous Allied prisoners to safety through enemy lines by liaising the 8th^a Army Command with bases in Marche and Abruzzi. Wanted by the Nazi-Fascists, he was captured in an ambush, subjected to threats and torture and finally shot.

36 Intelligence School 9, called 'A' Force on that front, its officers were assigned to No. 5 Field Section, operating east along the Adriatic coast and commanded by Capt Andrew George Robb (born 20.03.1901 in Dunedin, New Zealand). The duties of IS9 were: interrogate escapees and evaders (E & E s) once they had returned, instruct and brief Imperial and American personnel on the conduct to be followed by prisoners of war as well as escape and evasion, provide tools and devices to escape and evade capture, rescue by any means except arms all E & Es, report to the authorities E & Es deserving of honours and those whose actions are considered adverse to the Armed Forces, give rewards to civilian aides who have assisted E & Es and reported crimes on them.

▲ At 11.35 a.m. on 12.08.1942, the S. 79 of the 258th Aero Squadron of the 109th Group left Decimo (Decimomannu N.A.) for a

[...] Torpedo action against a British naval convoy consisting of 2. aircraft carriers - 2. battleships - 6. cruisers 14 C.C.T.s and an unknown number of steamers - violent anti-aircraft reaction - violent air reaction. Resulting affon. from the massed action of the apparatus - 2 steamers and one light warship - hit - one battleship - 3 Cruisers and 2 Steamers. Fights were sustained against enemy fighters. Resulted in being shot down - 3 Hurricanes plus one probable - our app. did not return. The app. returned hit. Duration 125', altitude 800, arrival at Decimo at 13.40 (photo taken from Personal flying logbook of airman chosen assistant airman Sobatti Carlo, op. cit. in bibliography).

decided to join the Aeronautica Nazionale Repubblicana or ANR *N.d.A.*) and the 28th Bombardment Group, moved south and reconstituted the 132nd Group at Galatina Airport (LE), which later became part of the "Stormo Baltimore[37] " of the Italian Co-belligerent Air Force (ICAF) based at Campo Vesuvio[38]. Carlo Winspeare, continued the war employed on in-

---

37 On 1 July 1944, the 'Baltimore Wing' was officially established at the Campo Vesuvio base, which took charge of the Martin 187 *Baltimore* aircraft. The personnel were volunteers and comprised about 630 men between the navigating and ground services roles from the 132nd Transport Group, which in turn had originated from the 41st Aerosilurant Group, the 104th Aerosilent Group and the 132nd Aerosilent Group. The unit consisted of two groups, the first led by Maj. Erasi and the second by Maj. Buscaglia, who, after two years of captivity, was immediately given command. The unit was then transferred to Campomarino (CB) in November 1944, from where it operated for war activity as part of the *Balkan Air Force* under the RAF's 254 *Wing* in the Adriatic theatre, with missions directed towards the Balkans and the Istrian coast. Today, the 132nd Reconnaissance Bomber Fighter Group is an Air Force flight group attached to the 51st Wing.
38 Campo Vesuvio, in the province of Naples, was a temporary airfield built by the Anglo-Americans in an agricultural area about 2 km east of the towns of San Giuseppe Vesuviano and Ottaviano. They employed it for a short time while they restored the runway at Capodichino, damaged by their own bombing. It was built by the XII *Engineering Command* of the *Twelfth Air Force* using the then customary technique of compressing the ground and covering it with metal elements, called 'grelle', which were profiled and drilled. The flooring extended to the taxiing areas and the structure was completed with tents for the crews and technicians. The metal floor, however, quickly wore out the tyres and was often uneven, all made worse by the soil, made of fine volcanic pumice dust, which rose under the movement of the propellers causing

▲ Photo taken, perhaps, at Pantelleria: under the central propeller of an S. 79, Carlo Winspeare (right) appears to be talking to Ugo Rivoli (left) and a non-commissioned officer (centre). Note the badge for the crews of the Aerosiluranti, sewn onto the flight jacket of 'ours' (photo g.c. Collection Edoardo Winspeare).

▶ "Pik As ist Trumpf" was the motto that appeared on some of the *Jagdgeschwader* 53's aircraft of which, not surprisingly, the ace of spades was the symbol. On 12 August 1942, its Bf 109s took part in the Battle of Mid-August together with the 132nd Autonomo Aerosilurant Group and other Italian-German airborne units (photo taken from https://commons.wikimedia.org/).

telligence missions with the British 'A' Force (which also dealt with disinformation *N.d.A.*) as an informer on German troop movements beyond the *Gustav* Line (which he crossed several times, especially in the first period of its operation *N.d.A.*), a fortified defensive line built by the Germans that started from the mouth of the Garigliano river and reached the coastal town of Ortona, dividing Italy in two: to the north the territory controlled by the Italian Social Republic and the Germans, to the south the territory in Allied hands. In her diaries, Countess Vinci Gigliucci recounts:

> [...] by the gentle and poetic Carlo Winspeare, with a face of a boy not yet of age and a head so in the clouds - at least in appearance - that he would hardly have attracted the suspicions of the Nazi-Fascists.

Having arrived in Bari, it seems that 'ours' resumed his position as a pilot in the Regia Aeronautica which, in the meantime, had become the ICAF. On 30 September 1943, he reported to Gioia del Colle Airport (BA). He was then at the Nucleo Aeronautica Campania Command at 3ª RAF Air Base[39] in Portici (NA) from 20 October 1943. On 15 February 1944, he was placed on leave and assigned to the Comando Nucleo Aeronautica Campania. During the war of liberation, he belonged to Commands, Agencies, Service Departments that were mobilised and in the area of operations from 30 September 1943 to 14 February 1944. On 6 April 1945, Carlo Winspeare wrote a letter, the full text of which is given below:

Naples 6-IV-45

The undersigned presents the following:

he is the owner of three houses ("Villa Salve", Piazza S. Stefano 6 and Via S. Stefano 4 and 3; the latter house is still requisitioned but not actually occupied) requisitioned by the Special Corps (Piazza S. Stefano 6) and 401 Signals (Via S. Stefano 3 and 4). Since he is obliged by these circumstances to live in only one room, and since he does not have a room for his work (biological research), he would like at least one room to be released from requisition in Via S. Stefano 4 and a storage room in the same house. The room he would like to have released from seizure is the last one with the fireplace. The name of the commanding officer of the unit currently occupying his house is Lt Col H. M. Kirkaldy Via Tasso 315.

Cordially

Dr. Carlo Winspeare

'Villa Salve'

Via S. Stefano 4

Naples

It is likely that 'ours', apart from the inconvenience of having to live in only one room and not having enough space for biological research, wanted his dwelling released because he was to marry the woman he loved within a few months. But the response from the *Headquarters Allied Military Government* was as follows:

Headquarters

Allied Military Government

Municipality of Naples

21 April 1945

---

damage to the engines and mechanical parts of the aircraft.
39 No. 3 Base Personnel Depot Portici, Naples.

Subject: Requisitioned property. 401 BR. SIG. ORGA.
A: Carlo Winspear,
  Piazzetta S. Stefano 6 and Via S. (Stefano 3 and 4 *N.d.A.*), Naples.
1. With reference to your request dated 6 April 1945.
2. We regret that it is impossible to release your property at this time.
For the Commissioner:

LAWRENCE E. KEARIN,
Infantry captain,
Helper.

At that time, release was not possible 'for reasons of overcrowding regarding the first unit, and security regarding the other'.

At the end of the war, on 8 August 1945, the Ministerial Commission for Personnel (which had jurisdiction over purges, *ed.*) of the Ministry of the Air Force, recorded the examination of Second Lieutenant A.A.r.n. pilot Winspeare Carlo of 57^a Squadron BT Jesi Airport, who had meanwhile established his residence in Depressa (LE), noting the

[...] Behaviour at the armistice and in the days immediately afterwards in relation to enemy oppression:

He walked away from the Jesi airport and crossed the (enemy *N.A.*) lines.

Conduct in the subsequent period, i.e. of the establishment of the republican government, until the day of the liberation of the place of residence or service:

He presented himself to the legitimate authorities on 2.10.1943.

JUDGMENT:

Category: 1st - (First)

Therefore, on 5 September 1945, the Undersecretary of State in the Minister's Office, Ernesto Pellegrino, in agreement, ascribed the officer to the 1^a category.

From 31 March 1946, he was in force at the Nucleus 3 Command^a ZAT due to a change of territorial jurisdiction. On 11 February 1952, he was promoted to lieutenant, with seniority in rank starting on 31 December 1945, although the personal report on his suitability for promotion, signed by the Commander of 57^a Squadron, pilot Captain Viviano Baronti, is dated 18 April 1943:

[...] Healthy and robust despite his slender constitution, he is resistant to the exertions of flight and field work, even in poor living conditions. He has a passion for sports in general, especially skiing; he can swim. He is a serious young man of quick intelligence and good will; with a degree in natural sciences, he has a vast and profound culture, superior to his rank, which he is constantly improving and increasing through systematic study. He knows English and French well, German less so. His technical and professional knowledge is also very good and his Air Force culture, marked and clear, makes him stand out and emerge among the officers held. He knows how to make himself loved by his inferiors, whom he treats with proper discernment. Respectful towards his superiors, he carries out the orders entrusted to him with promptness, acumen and willingness and knows how to win their sympathy. He served in a torpedo bomber squadron where as a crew chief he carried out three reconnaissance flights along the Tunisian coast and six convoy escorts. As second pilot he took part in the Battle of Mid-August (12-13 August 1942) earning the Bronze Star Medal 'in the field'. Although he did not have many flying hours, S. Lieutenant Winspeare proved to be an excellent pilot and an

▲ A 'cursed hunchback' (bombing version), with three-blade propellers; the ventral nacelle can be distinguished and the attachments for the two torpedoes are missing, flying over the heavily armed British base in Malta. Initially, the aircraft was equipped with Piaggio P.XI radial engines, which were replaced by three Alfa Romeo 126 RC.34 radial engines with 750 hp and, later, Alfa Romeo 128 RC.18 with 860 hp each (photo taken from *7 Years of War, photo-history of the Second World War as seen by the two warring sides*, op. cit. in bibliography).

▼ "Picchiatelli" or Ju. 87 *Stuka* of the 239th Autonoma Tuffer Squadron of the 102nd Group filmed during the Battle of Pantelleria. The aircraft in the foreground has the silhouettes of the (presumed) sunken ships and the serial number drawn on the drift; on the right, in the background, two FIAT CR42 "Falco" can be recognised. The aircraft of the 102nd Group also participated in the Battle of Mid-August (photo taken from *Aerei italiani contro navi inglesi*, op. cit. in bibliography).

▲ The torpedo bomber Carlo Winspeare (left) ready to leave for a war mission in the Central Mediterranean (photo Luce, taken from Stampa Sera, op. cit. in bibliography).

▼ After an attack manoeuvre, an S.M. S. 79 torpedo bomber version flies at low altitude over a British ship, countered by a heavy anti-aircraft barrage, note the torpedo still attached to the aircraft's 'belly' and the wing cockades with the lictor beams of recognition (author's photo).

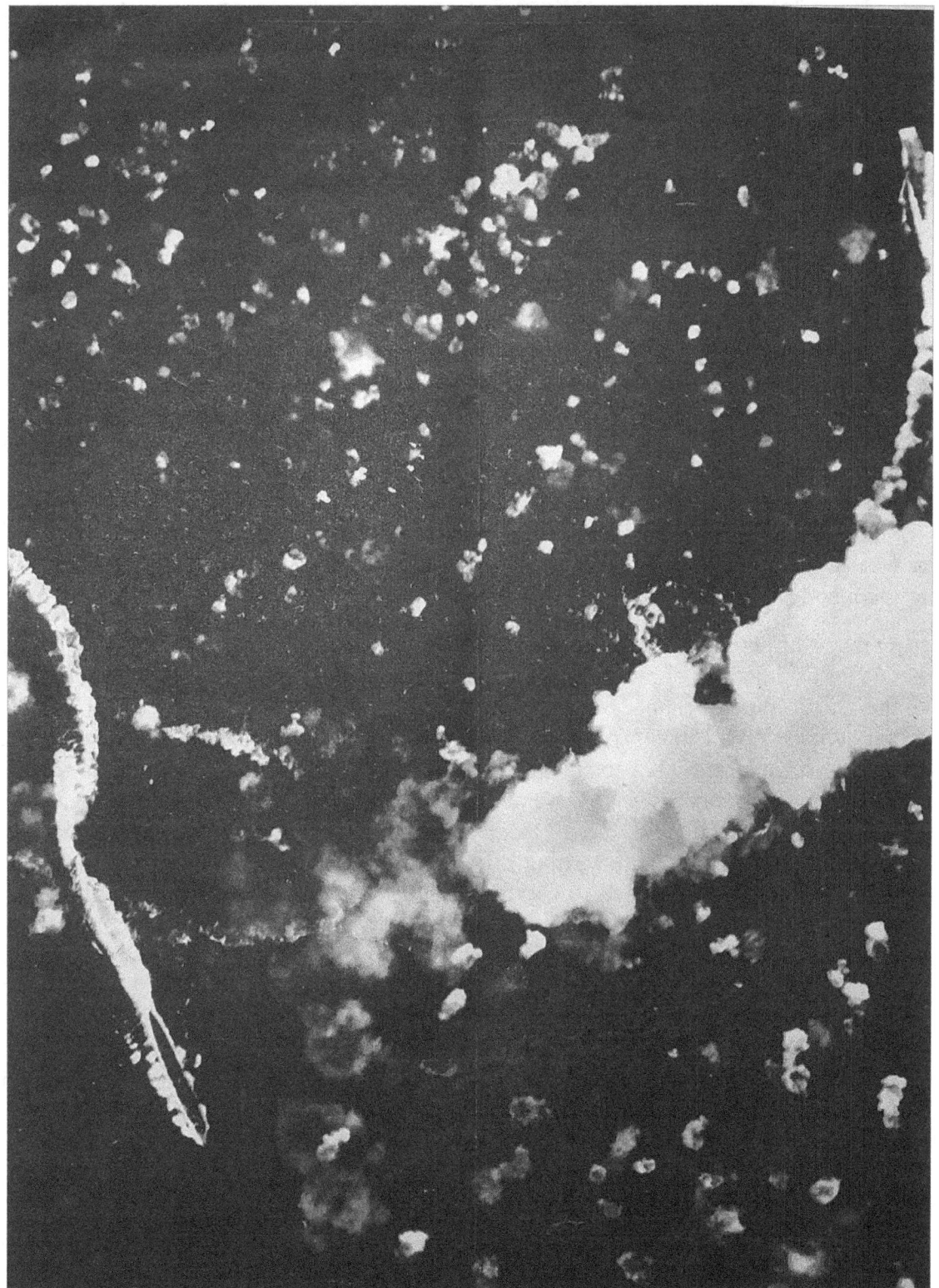

▲ The infernal anti-aircraft barrage did not stop the momentum of the attacking Italian aircraft. A column of smoke appears to rise from an aircraft carrier (photo taken from *La Battaglia del Canale di Sicilia, Mezz'agosto 1942-XX*, op. cit. in bibliography).

able patrolman full of passion for flying and a willingness to learn. Good comrades towards his colleagues, friendly and jovial with everyone. Gifted with initiative and a sense of responsibility, I consider S. Lt. WINSPEARE SUITABLE for promotion to a higher rank (op. cit.).

These words denote, without a shadow of a doubt, the maturity of character and improved military skills he had acquired. But how come 'our' was promoted almost 7 years after the end of the war? Undoubtedly the wartime events unfavourable to Italy had a certain weight. An explanation can still be found in the words of his nephew Edward:

[...] As chance would have it, forty years later, I had his marconist as a mathematics teacher at the high school (Barnabiti in Florence, *ed.*). When on the first day of school, Professor Mici - that was his name - scrolled through the list of students with his head bent over the register, read my surname, looked up and, seriously, asked me if I was related to Commander Carlo Winspeare. When he got confirmation that I was his nephew, he promised me years of hell: "Your uncle was a madman who only released the torpedo when he was very close to the enemy ship. We were terrified and shouted at him to take off again to escape the close anti-aircraft gunfire, but he wanted to be sure to hit the ship". In my naivety as a teenager, I really thought that, almost half a century later, the professor wanted to make me pay for my uncle's reckless ventures. A few moments passed, the grim look dissolved into a smile: "But after all I loved him..." Luckily he was joking, and on the contrary, he always promoted me 'for war merits', despite the fact that I was a disaster in mathematics, such was the esteem and affection towards his pilot commander... I wonder if his excessive actions were a way of exorcising death. (op. cit.).

Perhaps 'his uncle's reckless ventures' were the cause of his non-promotion, despite the heroic deeds described above. On 16 October 1951, he was transferred to the Command of the 4ª ZAT due to a change of residence, then on 22 June 1956 he returned to the Command of the 3ª ZAT. Having completed his 35th year of age, he remained, upon request, in the Air Force, sailor role (12 September 1961). On 5 April 1967, he was transferred, with his own rank and seniority (since 31 December 1945), to the reserve complementary category, due to age limit, effective 14 March 1962. On 24 October of the same year, the Ministerial Decree dated 5 April 1967 concerning his placement in the complementary reserve was revoked, and he was promoted to Captain with seniority as of 31 December 1956, and then transferred again, with his own rank and seniority, to the category of complementary reserve, due to age limit, as of 14 March 1962 (as above). On 1 July 1969, he was promoted to the rank of 1st Captain, and from 5 November 1970, he was on duty at the 3ª Air Region Command due to a change of residence (he lived in Depressa, in the province of Lecce, *editor's note*). On 24 August 1972, he was decorated for requirements with the Croce al Merito di Guerra (1940 - 1945 campaign, 1ª concession). On 15 December 1978, he was placed on absolute leave due to age, effective 14 March 1979. This is how Martino Aichner, a friend of his from his flying school days and ward comrade, described Carlo Winspeare:

[...] A few days later, two more[40] classmates were assigned to our department: Carletto Winspeare from Naples... with noble blood emerging from his thin skin, he still lives in Naples and, five decades later, has not aged in his indefinable age and enthusiasm. Generous and gentlemanly, he was and remains a dear friend to each and every one of us. (Aichner, Martino - Evangelisti, Giorgio, Storia degli aerosiluranti italiani e del gruppo Buscaglia, Milan, Longanesi, 1969).

---

40 The other officer was second lieutenant pilot Mario Mazzocca from Tripoli.

▲ General view of the convoy bound for Malta under air attack showing the intense anti-aircraft barrage from the escort ship and merchant ships. On the left the battleship *HMS Rodney*, on the right the cruiser *HMS Manchester* (photo Roper, F. G., taken from https://commons.wikimedia.org/).

After the war, he married Donna Maria Vittoria Colonna dei Principi di Stigliano[41] on 11 July 1945. A loyal and convinced supporter of the monarchy, he regarded communism[42] as 'smoke in the eyes'. During the electoral campaign for the referendum on the institutional form of the state in 1946, he tore down pro-republic posters and his wife even had to fetch him from the police station for fighting with supporters of the other faction.

[...] For many years after the war, he tempted fate by flying small touring planes with half-empty fuel tanks, for the gamble of landing with the engines off once the fuel ran out (op. cit.).

Perhaps he lacked the reckless ventures of yore: 'Boys, let's see how many red lights we

---

41 Maria Vittoria Colonna (27.09.1915-14.09.2011), always an elegant woman, came from one of the oldest families in Italy. Already accustomed to life with the military (her father, Giuliano, was a lieutenant in the cavalry during the Great War and decorated with the MBVM, her brother Landolfo was promoted for war merits in East Africa), she married Carlo Winspeare even though she knew that her future husband could never become a father. She stood by him and loved him tenderly even after he left home. Between the 1970s and 1980s, for 15 long years, she lived alone on the Fano farm near Salve (LE) without running water and electricity, surrounded by artists from all over Europe and the United States, to whom she had lent her haystacks near the Fano stream to create the utopian Fano Foundation. Maria Vittoria had become the patroness of counterculture artists from the 1960s and, in general, free spirits who sought a more authentic relationship with the land and people. Among them are the sculptor Norman Mommens and the writer Patience Gray.
42 Marquise Maria Vittoria 'Tini' Guillion Mangilli (born Winspeare, Naples 04.01.1916 - Montebelluna 04.04.2011), Carlo Winspeare's cousin, on the other hand, worked as a relay girl on Monte Grappa with the partisans of the Matteotti Brigade. In 1944 she was captured and put to the wall twice... She was saved from the death sentence thanks to her sister Adriana's friendship with Junio Valerio Borghese, the Commander of the X^a MAS.

can get through today...'. (op. cit.) was the phrase he used to say to his grandchildren, still children, when he secretly loaded them into the car. He amused himself by frightening passers-by by grazing them as he ran with the car, by driving his car into the still smouldering tar and drawing an '8' or an 'S' with the wheels, which sent him into raptures' (while the construction workers chased him, Ed.), firing firecrackers on New Year's Eve aroused his hilarity and when he went to Apulia to visit his brother Riccardo 'Dicky', he would punctually break the gearbox at Ariano Irpino (AV), who knows why...

[...] Among his many extravagances was the nudism he ... practised on the beach since the 1930s. You can imagine the scandal among bathers at that time in southern Italy (op. cit.).

An ingenious, kind-hearted (also confirmed by the writer's father *N.d.A.*) and sympathetic man, from an early age he showed a penchant for scientific subjects. A telecommunications enthusiast and radio amateur, in his youth he managed to assemble a radio and, later, a television set (but with exposed wires *N.d.A.*), participated in the construction of grandiose works such as the Monte Vergine (AV) transmitter centre and several radio bridges, published scientific articles and translated texts on the same subject from English such as "The Chromosomes of Michael J. D. White"[43] (translation in the second English edition). He managed to install a telephone in a car, something revolutionary for the time in which he conceived it! However, he was unable to match two socks of the same colour or a pair of shoes and happened to comb his hair only on one side. A clear example of genius and unruliness. He loved the poor, those who lived in the 'lowlands' of Naples and could not afford a normal meal, so it was no surprise to see some of them sitting at the table with him, brought in unexpectedly, without informing his wife and the service staff who would do their best, even improvising, to welcome guests. He often placed himself at the centre of female interest, which was reciprocated with the same enthusiasm, thanks also to his reputation as a heroic pilot. Deeply religious and a practising Catholic, he always carried the miraculous medal with him on missions. He was also an ardent devotee of Padre Pio of Pietrelcina (whose 'perfume' *he* could smell), to whom he went for confession, perhaps out of a desire to atone for sins committed during the war. "He remained an eccentric idealist, an emulation of Saint Francis" (op. cit.) and when someone reminded him of his noble origins, he replied that "octopuses have blue blood". He died in Cavriago in the province of Reggio Emilia on 7 November 2009[44] leaving his legacy to the family of a mystic who had been nourished for years by the consecrated host, who also came from the land of the Saint. In the past, a pilot like Carlo Winspeare was called the 'Ace of Aviation', today we will say that he attended the US combat school for pilots nicknamed 'Top Gun', but for me he was and always will be Blue Baron. Blue like his uniform, like the colour of his city and like the sky in which he loved to fly.

---

43 Michael James Denham White (London 10.08.1910 - Canberra 16.12.1983), grew up in Tuscany where he was home-schooled before beginning his university studies at University College London where he became a lecturer in zoology. He was then Professor of Zoology at the University of Texas and Professor of Genetics at the University of Melbourne. He finished his career at the Australian National University. In 1961 he was elected a Fellow of the Royal Society and was awarded the Linnean Medal in 1983. His work contributed to the development of cytology, cytogenetics and speciation.
44 According to other sources, he died in Naples on 7 November 2008.

▲ The air-sea battle of the Mediterranean on 11-15 August 1942. 'Dense columns of black smoke began to rise from the sea, covered in fuel slicks'. Note, left, the wing of the aircraft from which the action was filmed (photo taken from *La Battaglia del Canale di Sicilia, Mezz'agosto 1942-XX*, op. cit. in bibliography).

Report Executed in the waters off the Isle of Dogs on 12 August 1942 XX°

ATTACKING AIRCRAFT CREW

1)	Capitano Pil.	RIVOLI	Ugo	2)	Tenente Pil.	BARGAGNA	Francesco
	S. Tenente "	ANGELUCCI	Ramiro		Serg. M. "	MOSCHI	Sesto
	Maresc. Marc.	BALESTRI	Edmondo		I° Av. Marc.	CIANFARANI	Aldo
	I° Av. Mot.	PASTORI	Nello		Av. Sc. Mot.	SIROTTI	Eno
	Serg. M. Arm.	CORBU	Salvatore		I° Av. Arm.	SCATTIGNA	Francesco
					Av. Sc. Fot.	LUCARINI	Alberico
3)	Tenente Pil.	BARANI	Guido	4)	S. Tenente Pil.	MORETTI	Vittorio
	Serg. M. "	MAVILIO	Fernando		Serg. M. "	ZASA	Fulvio
	I° Av. Mot.	FRANCO	Italo		I° Av. Mot.	SAVIO	Guido
	I° Av. Marc.	DI MEGLIO	Alfredo		I° Av. Arm.	TARTAGLIONE	Giuseppe
	Av. Sc. A. Arm.	RIGUCCI	Pietro		Av. Sc. Marc.	CARIDDI	Franco
	Av. All. Fot.	FERRARI	Vittorio		I° Av. Fot.	BELLICONI	Settimio
5)	S. Tenente Pil.	PFISTER	Carlo	6)	S. Tenente Pil.	MAZZOCCA	Mario
	Serg. M. "	TEOTINO	Ilario		Serg. Magg. "	CAPOGROSSI	Giuseppe
	Serg. M. Mot.	BARENGHI	Luigi		I° Av. Mot.	CERBONCINI	Fosco
	I° Av. Arm.	D'ANGELO	Salvatore		I° Av. Arm.	MANGANO	Enrico
	I° Av. Marc.	SANTINELLO	Alfredo		Av. Sc. Marc.	MALARA	Francesco
7)	S. Tenente Pil.	COCI	Giuseppe	8)	Capitano Pil.	GRAZIANI	G. Cesare
	Serg. M. "	OLIVIERO	Andrea		Maresc. "	MARGUTTI	Gildo
	Av. Sc. Mot.	BUSETTO	Luigi		I° Av. Mot.	TAMBURINI	Luigi
	Av. Sc. Marc.	CATALANO	Alberto		Serg. Marc.	CASELLATO	Renzo
	Av. Sc. A. Arm.	SCIBINICO	Giuseppe		I° Av. Arm.	GIANANDREA	Italo
					I° Av. Fot.	CUPIRAGGI	Francesco
9)	Tenente Pil.	FAGGIONI	Carlo	10)	Tenente Pil.	MARINI	Marino
	S. Ten. "	WINSPEARE	Carlo		Serg. M. "	BORGHI	Armando
	Serg. M. Mot.	FACCA	Ideale		Maresc. Mot.	SACCHI	Augusto
	Av. Sc. Marc.	CAPALDI	Giovanni		Av. Sc. Marc.	PICERNO	Mario
	I° Av. Arm.	GIANNI	Italo		Av. Sc. Arm.	ANDREANI	Giuseppe
	Av. Sc. Fot.	DANIELLO	Loreto		Av. Sc. Fot.	VASCELLARI	Ugo
11)	Tenente Pil.	VINCIGUERRA	Pasquale	12)	S. Ten. Pil.	AICHNER	Martino
	Serg. M. "	ROSCINI	Italo		Serg. M. "	SOGLIUZZO	Francesco
	Av. Sc. Mot.	FANTUZZI	Massimil.		Av. Sc. Mot.	TORELLO	Gino
	Av. Sc. Marc.	PETRAROLI	Antonio		Av. Sc. Marc.	DI DARIO	Guido
	I° Av. Arm.	ARRIGANELLO	Pietro		Av. Sc. Arm.	DE SANTIS	Fausto
					Av. Sc. A. Fot.	CERRATO	Mario
13)	Tenente Pil.	MANFREDI	Paolo	14)	Tenente Pil.	MIGLIACCIO	Aldo
	Serg. M. "	BERNARDI	Luigi		Serg. M. "	DEL BIANCO	Oreste
	I° Av. Mot.	BERTOLINA	Giulio		Av. Sc. Mot.	MONDELLO	Salvatore
	Av. Sc. Marc.	BENETOLLO	Vinicio		Av. Sc. Marc.	MEOZZI	Menotti
	I° Av. Arm.	AGOSTA	Saverio		I° Av. Arm.	DEL PRETE	Sossio
	Av. Sc. Fot.	CARINGELLA	Giuseppe		Av. All. A. Fot.	DE MATTEIS	Cesare

| FALLEN* OF THE R. AIR FORCE DURING THE BATTLE OF MID-AUGUST 1942 |

Rank	Name	Surname	Aircraft	Group	Squadron	Date
Ten. Pil.	Silvio	ANGELUCCI	S. 79 Sil.	105°	255ª	13.08.1942
Ten. Pil.	Guido	BARANI	S. 79 Sil.	132°	278ª	13.08.1942
Ten. Pil.	Alfonso	BATTISTINI	S. 79 Sil.	30°	56ª	14.08.1942
I° Av. Mot.	Giuseppe	CALORENNA	Ju. 87	102°	239ª	12.08.1942
Serg. Pil.	Ugo	CASAVOLA	Ju. 87	102°	239ª	12.08.1942
Serg. Pil.	Giulio	CREMONESI	Ju. 87	102°	239ª	12.08.1942
S. Ten. Pil.	Michele	CRIMI	Re. 2001	2°	362ª	12.08.1942
S. Ten. Pil.	Alessandro	DELLA BARBA	S. 84	38°	50ª	
S. Ten. Pil.	Tullio	DESSÌ	S. 84	38°	50ª	
Ten. Pil.	Bartolomeo	FERRANTE	S. 79	32°	58ª	13.08.1942
Av. All. Fot.	Vittorio	FERRARI	S. 79 Sil.	132°	278ª	13.08.1942
I° Av. Mot.	Italo	FRANCO	S. 79 Sil.	132°	278ª	13.08.1942
Ten. Pil.	Italo	MASINI	Cant. Z. 1007bis	33°	59ª	13.08.1942
Serg. M. Pil.	Fernando	MAVILIO	S. 79 Sil.	132°	278ª	13.08.1942
Cap. Pil.	Giovanni	MOLLO	S. 79	32°	57ª o 58ª	--.08.1942
S. Ten. Pil.	Vittorio	MORETTI	S. 79 Sil.	132°	278ª	12.08.1942
Ten. Pil.	Vittorio Emanuele	OTTAVIANI	Cant. Z. 1007	51°	212ª	
Av. All. Mot.	Giovanni	PARIETTI	Ju. 87	102°	239ª	12.08.1942
I° Av. Marc.	Tullio	PEDEMONTE	S. 79 Sil.	132°	278ª	13.08.1942
Serg. M. Pil.	Oscar	RAIMONDO	Ju. 87	102°	239ª	13.08.1942
Ten. Col. Pil.	Ivo	RAVAZZONI	S. 84	25°	9ª	14.08.1942
Serg. Marc.	Pasquale	ROMBOLÀ	S. 79 Sil.	109°	258ª o 259ª	
Magg. Pil.	Pier Giuseppe	SCARPETTA	Re. 2001	2°	150ª	14.08.1942
Av. Sc. Mot.	Aldo	TARABOTTI	Ju. 87	102°	239ª	13.08.1942
I° Av. Arm.	Giuseppe	TARTAGLIONE	S. 79 Sil.	132°	278ª	13.08.1942
S. Ten. Pil.	Renato	TOSI	B.R. 20	88°	264ª	14.08.1942
Magg. Pil.	Alfredo	ZANARDI	S. 79	109°	258ª o 259ª	--.08.1942

* To the casualties listed above must be added the 2 soldiers who died as a result of the *Beaufighter* machine-gunning action on the airports of Elmas and Decimomannu at dusk on 11.08.1942.

▲ The commander of the 281st Squadron, pilot captain Giulio Cesare Graziani (24.01.1915-23.12.1998), grandson of Marshal Rodolfo of Italy, after the shooting down of Buscaglia in the Bougie roadstead, became the acting commander of the 132nd Autonomous Aerosilhouette Group (photo taken from http://www.istitutodelnastroazzurro.org).

▲ Lieutenant-Pilot Carlo Faggioni (26.01.1915-10.04.1944) was the crew chief of the S. 79 on which Winspeare also boarded on 12 August 1942. After 8 September 1943, he joined the National Republican Air Force. He died during an attack action off the coast of Anzio (photo taken from https://commons.wikimedia.org/).

▲ S. 79 number 7 of the 281st Squadron, as can be seen from the numerals written on the fuselage, christened 'Faà di Bruno' in honour of Commander Emilio Faà di Bruno (07.03.1820-20.07.1866) who fell off the coast of Lissa. The photo, probably taken at the Pantelleria airfield in the summer of 1942, shows two crew members arguing at the boarding gate. According to some testimonies by former members of the unit, this is the aircraft that Faggioni often piloted, who, during the Battle of Mid-August, had Winspeare as his second pilot (photo taken from *Gli Aerosiluranti Italiani 1940-1945, I reparti, le macchine, le imprese*, op. cit. in bibliography).

▼ An S. 79 torpedo bomber positions itself to launch the torpedo it carries under the nacelle, the target is the warship in front of it. The fighters of the aircraft carrier in the background work to counter the torpedo bomber's pass (photo taken from *La Battaglia del Canale di Sicilia, Mezz'agosto 1942-XX*, op. cit. in bibliography).

▲ The British Royal Navy F-class destroyer *HMS Foresight* (H68) sunk on 13 August 1942 (photo Royal Navy, taken from https://commons.wikimedia.org/).

▼ Panoramic view during the course of the Mid-August Battle from the side machine-gun window, installed in the fuselage on a revolving support, of an S. 79; in the foreground, the collimator of the Breda-SAFAT (Società Anonima Fabbrica Armi Torino) 7.7 mm machine-gun that had to be aligned with the fixed sight (photo taken from *Documentary of the Mid-August Air and Sea Battle in the Central Mediterranean*, op. cit. in bibliography).

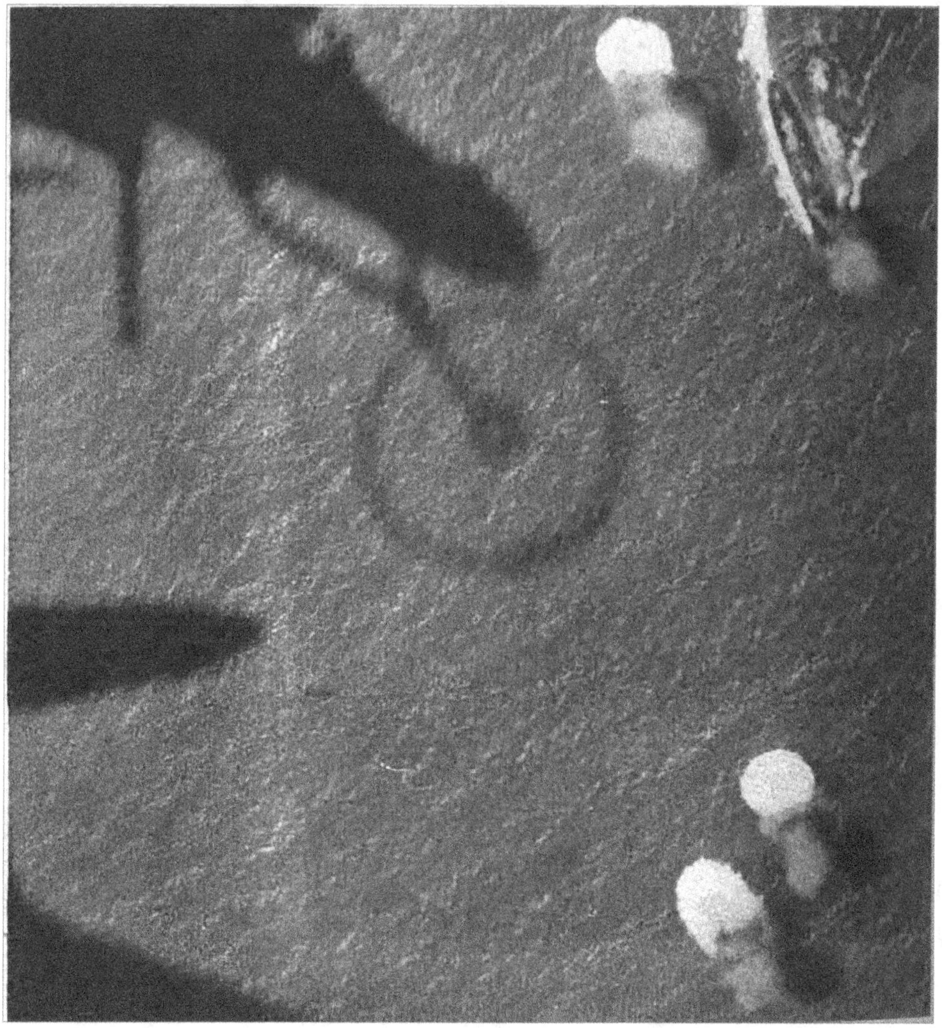

▲ A patrol of S.79 torpedo bombers prepares to 'launch' against the ships of the convoy bound for Malta (photo taken from *La Battaglia del Canale di Sicilia, Mezz'agosto 1942-XX*, op. cit. in bibliography).

▼ The Battle of the Sicilian Channel that took place from 11 to 15 August 1942. Flash of an explosion that appears to have occurred near the stern of a ship. (Istituto Luce photo, taken from: https://tecadigitaleacs.cultura.gov.it/).

▲ A destroyer, probably F-class, damaged in the bow area during the air-sea battle of 11-15 August 1942. Part of the stern seems to have been removed; therefore it was hit at least twice (photo taken from *La Battaglia del Canale di Sicilia, Mezz'agosto 1942-XX*, op. cit. in bibliography).

▼ HMS Foresight sank at 9.55 a.m. on 13 August 1942 off the coast of Bizerte at coordinates: 37°40' N 10°00' E (photo taken from https://www.google.it/).

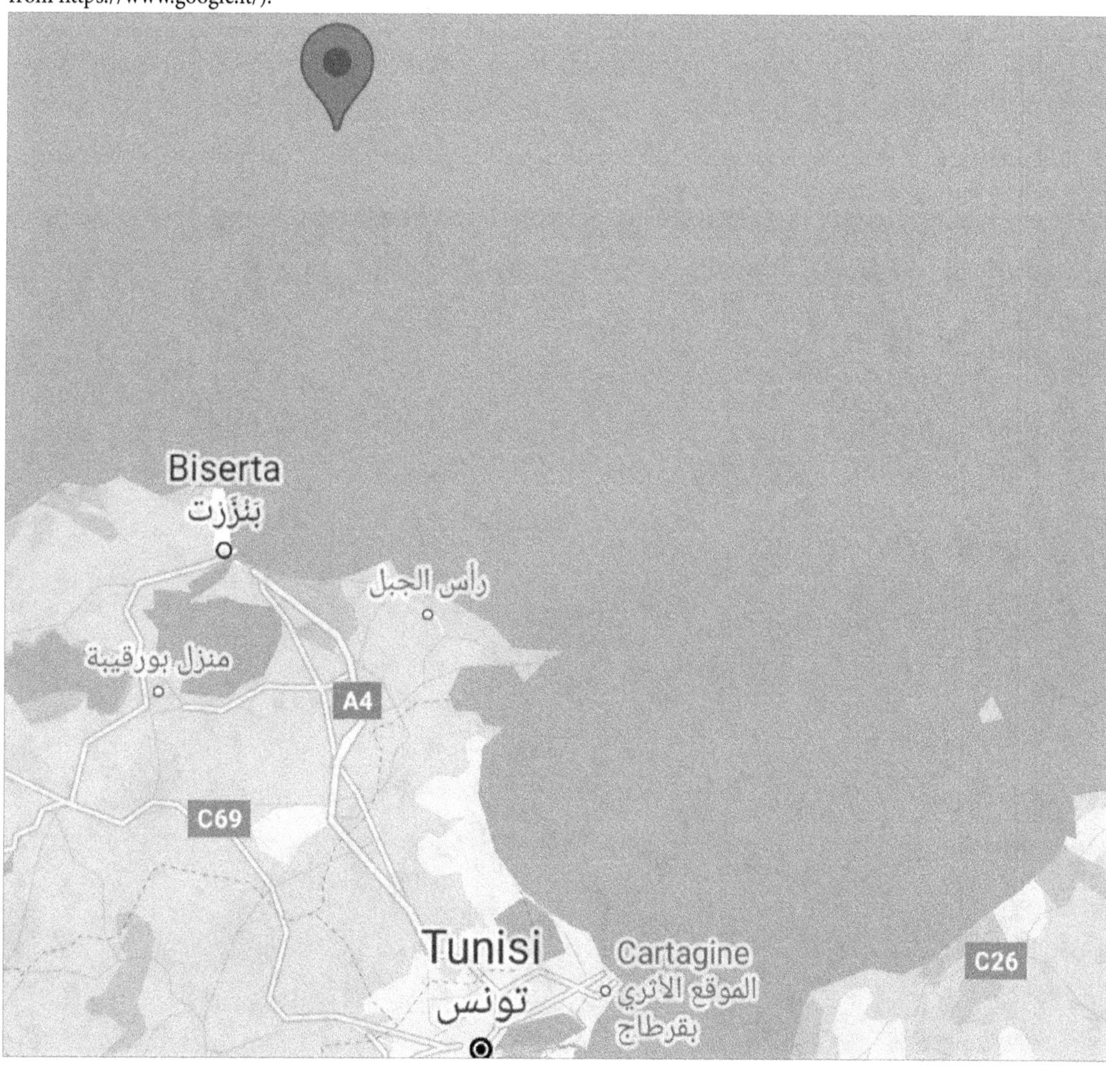

▲ The crew of an automatic anti-aircraft QF (which stands for 'quick firing') 2-pounder MK VIII 40 mm gun, also known as a multiple Pom-Pom, of a British destroyer enjoys a break during a lull in the action. How hard the British flak worked can be deduced from the amount of shells on the ship's deck and the faces of the soldiers (photo taken from *The Sphere*, op. cit. in bibliography).

▼ The Castelvetrano (TP) airfield, home of the 278th Squadron, seen from above in April 1942 (photo Royal Australian Air Force, taken from https://commons.wikimedia.org/).

▲ An S. 79 torpedo bomber jumps at an enemy unit (photo taken from La Battaglia del Canale di Sicilia, Mezz'agosto 1942-XX, op. cit. in bibliography).

▼ "At 11.20 a.m. on 13 August 1942 Italian torpedo bombers carried out a combined attack with the launching of parachute mines or torpedoes on a spiral course. The torpedoes were launched from long range except for one which caught on the paramine of *SS Port Chalmers*" (Syfret, E. N., Operation 'Pedestal', Supplement to The London Gazette of Tuesday, the 10th of August, 1948, op. cit. in bibliography; photo taken from https://collections.slq.qld.gov.au/).

▲ The aircraft torpedo caught on the SS *Port Chalmers*' paramine cable. The ship could not slow down to release the torpedo for fear it would explode against the side of the ship. Eventually the entire paramine was abandoned at sea and the torpedo exploded on the bottom without causing any damage (photo taken from https://commons.wikimedia.org/).

▲ An Italian bomber (right), which was attacking a British destroyer, was hit by the deadly fire of the ship's QF 2-pound Pom-Pom and resolutely tried to escape. A few minutes later the plane crashed into the sea in flames (photo taken from *The War In The Air* in 'The War Illustrated', No. 136, September 4, 1942 op. cit. in bibliography).

▼ No passing in the Mediterranean, The decimated British convoy (photo taken from *Il Piccolo*, op. cit. in bibliography).

▲ Oil tanker set on fire by Italian bombers off Cape Mustafà (Tunisia): the scene is filmed at close range (photo taken from *La Battaglia del Canale di Sicilia, Mid-August 1942-XX*, op. cit. in bibliography).

◄ Ober leutnant Karl-Erich Ritter, born 03.01.1921 in Frankfurt am Main, professional soldier of Küstenflieger Gruppe 806 1. Staff. (FPN: 31399), who went missing with his crew on 11.08.1942 after the Ju. 88A-4 in which he was flying was shot down by flak from HMS Victorious during an attempted attack in the course of Operation Pedestal (photo taken from *Vermisstenbildlisten, Suchdienst*, Deutsches Rotes Kreuz, 1957).

▲ Some of the 927 survivors of the HMS Eagle swim among the wreckage before being transferred aboard another escort ship that protected the large convoy bound for Malta. At the start of the war, the Eagle hunted for raiders in the Indian Ocean. Later, it joined the Mediterranean Fleet and its aircraft were used in operations off Tobruch and Fort Capuzzo, took part in the Battle of Calabria and conducted raids against Italian airfields. In 1941 she attacked German supply ships in the South Atlantic, but in 1942 she returned to the Mediterranean where she was sunk by U-boat U-73 (photo taken from *I Was There!* in '*The War Illustrated*', No. 137, September 18, 1942 op. cit. in bibliography).

▲ *Fl/Sgt* John Harold Tanner, born in Wellington, New Zealand, on 21.06.1920 (serial number: RNZAF 41960) of 126 Squadron, missing and later believed dead on 13.08.1942 in the Mediterranean Sea after his Spitfire VB (serial number: EP472) was shot down by a German Bf 109 fighter while on a reconnaissance mission west of Malta during Operation Pedestal (photo taken from *Auckland Weekly News*, 24.03.1943, p. 18).

▲ After the glittering air and sea victory in the Mediterranean. Above the annihilated British convoy roaring past the Italian squadrons (drawing A. Beltrame, taken from *La Domenica del Corriere, Illustrated supplement to the 'Corriere della Sera'*, op. cit. in bibliography).

▲ General Silvio Scaroni (12.05.1893 - 16.02.1977), with 26 confirmed victories in the First World War, is considered the second Italian aviation ace. During the Second World War he was the Commander of the Sicilian Air Force, but in 1943 he was dismissed from it because he was in conflict with Reichsmarschall Hermann Göring, Commander-in-Chief of the Luftwaffe, for not having provided sufficient support to the German Air Force in the attacks against Malta (photo taken from https://commons.wikimedia.org/).

Ufficiali, sottufficiali, graduati, marinai e avieri!

Nei giorni 11, 12, 13 agosto voi avete - dopo aspra battaglia - annientato le forze navali nemiche che avevano ancora una volta tentato di avventurarsi nel mare di Roma. ★ Il nemico di solito così reticente e tardivo è stato costretto - data la gravità della sua catastrofe - a confessare le perdite e a riconoscere la vostra splendente vittoria. ★ Schiantate dalle vostre bombe e dai vostri siluri, le sue navi giacciono in fondo al Mediterraneo. ★ I camerati germanici - in fraterna emulazione con voi - hanno giorno e notte combattuto al vostro fianco e inflitto al nemico colpi mortali.

UFFICIALI, SOTTUFFICIALI, GRADUATI, MARINAI E AVIERI!
Nel breve ciclo di due mesi voi avete piegato sino alla più cocente umiliazione l'orgoglio di quella che fu un giorno la dominatrice dei mari, ne avete diminuito prestigio e potenza. ★ Il popolo italiano è fiero di voi. ★ Saluto al Re!

Dal Quartier Generale delle Forze Armate 15 Agosto XX   **MUSSOLINI**

▲ The Duce's proclamation to the Navy and Air Force, from Armed Forces Headquarters, 15 August 1942 (photo taken from *La Battaglia del Canale di Sicilia, Mezz'agosto 1942-XX*, op. cit. in bibliography).

▼ The *Grand Harbour* of Valletta, the main port of the island of Malta, once a proud bastion of British power in the Mediterranean and an important base on the sea route to India (photo taken from Der Adler, op. cit. in bibliography).

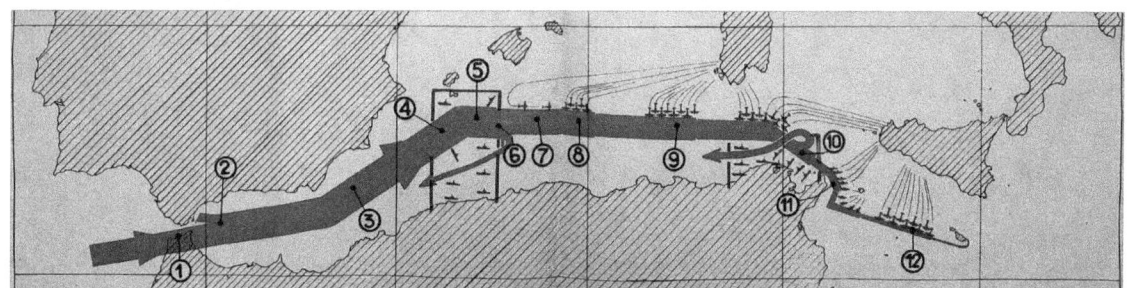

▲ On the night of 10 August 1942 a large convoy 1), coming from the Atlantic and bound for Malta, passed the Strait of Gibraltar and entered the Mediterranean. As it passed, the naval forces of Gibraltar 2) joined the convoy to reinforce its escort. During the night of 11 August, the massive complex headed north-east 3) to pass south of Ibiza of the Balearic Islands, in the western Mediterranean. At 04.38 on 11 August, the convoy was sighted 4), by the submarine Uarsciek, which attacked the aircraft carrier HMS Furious with three torpedoes, missing it. Around noon, it was the turn of the German submarine U-73 5), which hit the aircraft carrier Eagle with four torpedoes and sank her. A little later 6), the HMS Furious, laden with the shipwrecked HMS Eagle, reversed course and made her way back. During the day of the 11th, the convoy was followed by aerial reconnaissance 7) and at dusk suffered a first attack from Germanic aircraft 8). In the early morning hours of 12 August, the convoy was attacked by formations of Italian planes 9), which inflicted losses and heavy damage. At sunset and in the evening of the 12th, while part of the convoy reversed course to return to base, the convoy entered an ambush zone of submarines 10), which attacked it sinking other ships and hitting several. After passing Cape Bon, the convoy entered the ambush zone of the Mas 11), which, in attacks that lasted until dawn, sank and hit other units including the cruiser HMS Manchester, the steamers MV Glenorchy, SS Wairangi, SS Almeria Lykes, SS Rochester Castle, SS Santa Elisa. By the early morning hours of 13 August the surviving units were still being hit 12) by Italian and German aircraft, which sank other ships. Only four steamers and a tanker reached Malta (photo taken from *La Battaglia del Canale di Sicilia, Mezz'agosto 1942-XX*, op. cit. in bibliography).

▼ Crew of the aircraft, on which Carlo Winspeare was embarked, which on 12 August 1942, in the waters off the Isle of Dogs, attacked 'the most important merchant and war units of a mighty convoy coming from the west' (photo taken from the *Historical Diary* of the 132nd Torpedo Air Group, op. cit. in bibliography).

```
9) Tenente    Pil.   FAGGIONI   Carlo
   S.Ten.      "     WINSPEARE  Carlo
   Serg.M.    Mot.   FACCA      Ideale
   Av.Sc.     Marc.  CAPALDI    Giovanni
   1ºAv.      Arm.   GIANNI     Italo
   Av.Sc.     Fot.   DANIELLO   Loreto
```

> WINSPEARE Carlo, da La Valletta (Malta) - Sottotenente pilota.
>
> « Pilota di velivolo silurante partecipava a due successivi attacchi contro un convoglio nemico scortato da unità da guerra. Incurante della violentissima reazione contraerea e dei ripetuti attacchi della caccia avversaria, sganciava i siluri a breve distanza dagli obiettivi contribuendo ad affondare un incrociatore pesante ed a danneggiare altre unità da guerra e mercantili ».
>
> Cielo del Mediterraneo, 12-13 agosto 1942-XX

▲ The motivation for the first Military Valour Bronze Medal awarded to Second Lieutenant Pilot Winspeare Carlo (photo taken from Ministero dell'Aeronautica - Bollettino Ufficiale 1943 - Dispensa 14a - Onorificenze e Ricompense, p. 872).

▼ On the right, Second Lieutenant Pilot Carlo Winspeare (note the embroidered fabric badge for Aerosilurant crews sewn onto his flight jacket) from Naples, on the left Second Pilot Sergeant Armando Borghi (photo g.c. Collection Edoardo Winspeare).

▲ Carlo Winspeare, wearing a Saharan uniform, at an airfield. Behind him is a tent, probably assigned to airmen, and a wind-sleeve unfailing in an airport worthy of the name (photo g.c. Collection Edoardo Winspeare).

▲ Carlo Winspeare, photographed in uniform while reading a magazine of the time, appears to be sitting in a train, probably on leave. Note the pilot's badge, the eagle facing right surmounted by the crown, above the row of ribbons (photo g.c. Collection Edoardo Winspeare).

PROGRESS REPORT FROM NO. 5 FIELD SECTION
13 NOV 43.

Nov. 4. A sailing boat, bringing 5 ex-P/Ws, arrived TERMOLI from SAN BENEDETTO. This 'coup' had been successfully organised by Agent FAUSTO, of this Section, originally landed Oct 22, one of the six Agents who were working as a team (see Plan RATBERRY Section "A"). They were guided by FAUSTO and accompanied by two helpers. They brought a letter from FAUSTO assuring me that all had arrived safely, arranged r.v.s had been kept, and the Plan was going ahead. Good prospects are assured. The two Helpers will be returned to FAUSTO, as soon as possible.

Nov. 6. Took over officially from Col. WHYTE, and Section 5 now covers a 2 Divisional Front, Eight Indian Div, and 78 Div, moved to SAN FELICE.

Nov. 7. Contacted Capt. BRYANT, 8 Ind. Div., also Signals. Got latest 'dope' on how things are done, and got details re latest arrivals. Pte. JAMES WELLS, followed the popular route, towards PAIMOLI, passing through the hands of no fewer than 9 Helpers on route. Other ex-P/Ws tell of help by Parachutists, i.e. Maps, money, etc.

Nov. 8. "POP", a well-tried Agent, sent off across the lines, taking with him the two helpers who accompanied the five ex-P/Ws from SAN BENEDETTO. Contacted Intelligence Representatives of 78 Div. en route to 78 Div HQ. On his advice, the Div HQ being then on the move, did not go on, as nothing was likely to be accomplished. Sent on message by him to G.III(I) Capt. BIRD.

Nov. 9. Another Agent, has already done a job, sent over to contact "POP". HQ 8 Ind Div. moved forward to FURCI. During 9, 10, and 11 Nov on the 8 Ind Div. roads was almost impossible owing to the weather. Six hour halts were the usual thing, owing to the diversions being almost impassable, the roads being choked up with transport, in one case a 12 hr. block was experienced. I decided that it was better to be forward of Div. H.Q. and work across, so moved from PAIMOLI to CUPELLO.

Nov. 12. 2 Agents sent off from FURE, on the c.o.d. basis. Ex-P/Ws are passing through this Div Front at a steady pace. The majority have been given help on the other side. 44 have checked in since Nov 7.

Nov. 13. GALLEO, Agent making his 11th trip, sent off. This man does not work with directions given, but goes off on his own to his own contacts on the other side.
Returned to TERMOLI.
My chief Agent HUGH, head of the Original Six put in at CUPRA MARITIMA, reported back with full account of activities, Plan RATBERRY Section "A" and bringing with him 18 ex-P/Ws, 3 Helpers, and the following story.
"Following successful get-away of the five ex-P/Ws on Nov 4 it was decided to try it again. To keep 2 sailing vessels, which were about to sail, in abeyance, ERMANO, one of my original six, circulated the rumour that fishing vessels arriving at British Occupied Ports without some British P/W, were suspect. This had the desired result, and a promise

▲ 'A boat, carrying five former prisoners of war, arrived at Termoli from San Benedetto'. IS9 Progress Report from 4 to 21 November 1943 (photo g.c. Dennis Hill Collection).

▲ The Jesi airfield. On the eve of the last war, the old airfield was demolished and a military airport was built on its site. Due to the length of the runway (1,048 m × 60 m in macadam), the complex of barracks and hangars and the modernity of the facilities, it was considered the second in Italy. In 1943, there was a second-period flying school (BT speciality) with aircraft of the type B.R. 20 first and S.M. 79 later. In May of that year, 46 officers, 83 non-commissioned officers and 670 troops were on duty at the airport (photo g.c. Collection of the Little Jesina Library).

▶ Dino Philipson (26.09.1889-16.10.1972) one of the 5 'Argonauts' who, after 8 September, took part in the crossing from S. Benedetto del Tronto to Manfredonia. In February 1944, he became Undersecretary of State at the Presidency of the Council of Ministers in the Badoglio I government. Judged unreliable by the Allies, he continued in office thanks to the intervention of Violet Hoffnung. After the end of the war he was deputy to the National Council (photo taken from https://dati.camera.it/).

▶ The motivation for the Bronze Medal for Military Valour with which Carlo Winspeare was decorated for the second time (Ministry of Defence - Army - Official Bulletin - Dispensation 7a - Year 1949 - Rewards, p. 1294).

WINSPEARE Carlo fu Sarauw Clara, da La Valletta (Malta), classe 1917, sottotenente pilota arma aeronautica.
Sorpreso dagli avvenimenti dell'8 settembre 1943 in territorio occupato dai tedeschi, deciso a mettere la propria attività a servizio della Patria riusciva con quattro altri animosi ad impadronirsi di una motovedetta a servizio del nemico, a prendere il largo a S. Benedetto del Tronto in ora notturna ed a raggiungere il territorio liberato a Manfredonia all'alba successiva. La traversata protrattasi per 12 ore e rimessa alla sorte perchè erano privi di qualsiasi esperienza marinaresca, muniti di una semplice bussola di fortuna e dotati di limitata quantità di carburante. L'imbarcazione sottratta ai tedeschi veniva poi consegnata alla marina italiana. — Mare Adriatico, 8-9 settembre 1943.

▲ Uguccione Ranieri di Sorbello (22.02.1906-28.05.1969) in artillery lieutenant's outfit (c. 1928) another of the 5 'Argonauts' who, after 8 September, took part in the crossing from S. Benedetto del Tronto to Manfredonia. Between the winter of 1943 and the spring of 1944 he organised the Rat-Line in Marche territory, thanks to which hundreds of Allied prisoners were rescued (photo g.c. Photographic Archive Collection, Ranieri di Sorbello Foundation, Perugia via D. Brillini).

▲ Reserve cavalry colonel, army general staff, Giorgio Vicino Pallavicino (born 1879) was Andreola's father and the eldest of the five 'Argonauts' (photo taken from *I diari di Babka, 1943-1944 aristocrazia antifascista e missioni segreti*, op. cit. in bibliography).

▼ An S.M. 79 'Sparviero' of the Italian Co-belligerent Air Force or ICAF (Italian Co-belligerent Air Force) in southern Italy in 1943; the lictor recognition fasces were replaced by tricolour cockades following the RAF model (photo Spurr Algy, g.c. Brian Spurr Collection).

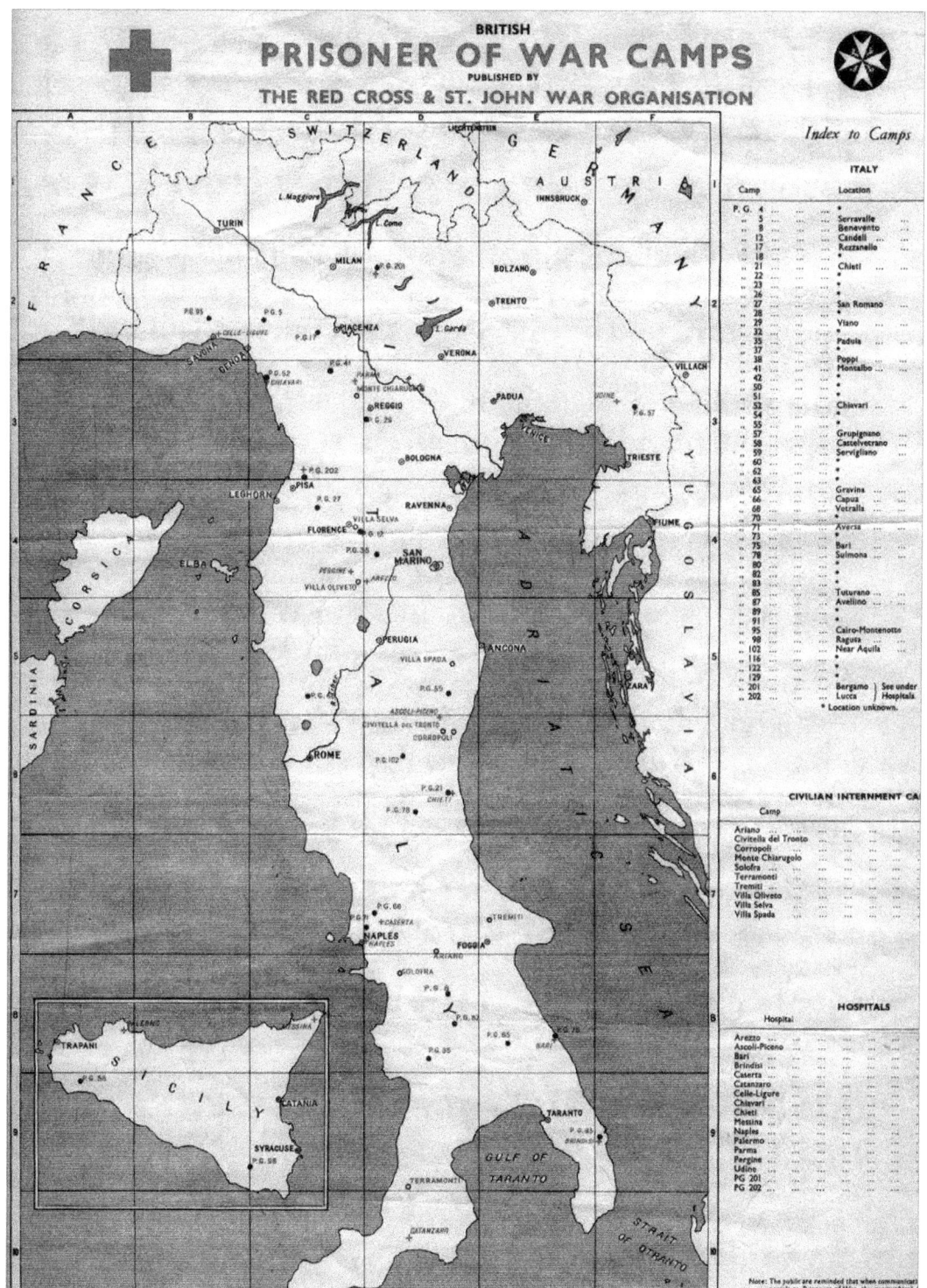

▲ The map, published by the Joint War Organisation of the British Red Cross and the Order of St. John (the latter also called the Order of Malta), shows the British prisoner-of-war camps in Italy as Campo per Prigionieri di Guerra 59 or PG59 in Servigliano (FM). Villa Boccabianca was one of the main bases of the 'Ratberry Line' or 'Rat-Line', used to free former prisoners of war (photo taken from https://museumandarchives.redcross.org.uk/).

ITALIANI!

Molti prigionieri inglesi e americani, riusciti a sfuggire dalle **mani dei Tedeschi** e a raggiungere l'Italia Libera, ci riferiscono di innumerevoli casi in cui amici italiani li hanno aiutati a sottrarsi al comune nemico, nascondendoli, fornendo loro cibo e vestiti e, infine, guidandoli verso la salvezza.

Il Governo Italiano, risoluto a proseguire, con ogni mezzo a sua disposizione, la guerra contro i Tedeschi, desidera che tutti gli Italiani sappiano che il patriottismo e la generosità di quanti aiutino soldati, aviatori e marinai inglesi o americani a rifugiarsi nell'Italia Libera, saranno ricompensati con un premio di lire cinque mila. Il premio sarà versato per tramite della Prefettura locale, non appena liberato dall'oppressore tedesco il territorio sotto la sua giurisdizione.

Abbiate cura di prender nota dei nomi e, possibilmente, dei numeri di matricola dei prigionieri inglesi e americani che salvate, assicurandovi che anche essi, a loro volta, abbiano i vostri nomi.

OGNI SOLDATO INGLESE O AMERICANO RESTITUITO ALLA LIBERTA, SIGNIFICA UN TEDESCO DI MENO

FUORI I TEDESCHI!

▲ Manifesto of the Italian Government with which it wished to let all Italians know that the patriotism and generosity of those who would help British or American soldiers, airmen and sailors to take refuge in Free Italy would be rewarded with a 5,000 Lire prize (photo taken from *I diari di Babka*, 1943-1944 aristocrazia antifascista e missioni segrete, op. cit. in bibliography).

▲ Fausto Simonetti (20.02.1921-06.06.1944), former Regia Aeronautica soldier, was commander of a partisan formation during the fighting at Colle San Marco. As an agent of IS9 (an emanation of the British Directorate of Military Intelligence Section 9 or MI9), also known as 'A' Force, he carried numerous Allied prisoners to safety across the Ratberry Line, taking care of the connection of the 8th Army Command with the bases in Marche and Abruzzi. Wanted by the Nazi-Fascists, he was captured and, subjected to threats and torture, shot (photo taken from https://www.movm.it).

▲ Captain Andrew George Robb (20.03.1901-_.12.1974), commander of No. 5 Field Section of IS9 or 'A' Force. On 2 November 1943, from Termoli, he landed four officers of Team Ratberry "A" (Uguccione Ranieri, "Don Carlo" Orlandini, Ermanno Finocchi and Andrea Scattini); on 3 November, they reached Post "A" (Villa Boccabianca in Cupra Marittima) where they joined Officer Fausto Simonetti who was waiting for them (photo g.c. Dennis Hill Collection).

▲ An S. 79 III Serie, without the targeting nacelle, belonging to the 2nd Squadron of the "Buscaglia" Group of the Aeronautica Nazionale Repubblicana (ANR), with a presumably dark green livery and the national symbols partially obliterated for night operations, prepares for a mission from the Lonate Pozzolo (VA) base. It is possible to make out the 'Republican' tricolour on the fuselage and two stylised lictor fasces delimited by a square on the wing of the aircraft (photo taken from *Regia Aeronautica, Vol. 2*, op. cit. in bibliography).

▼ The cockpit of a "Savoia-Marchetti" S. 79 aeroplane, the pilot's instrument panel and the engine control column are visible (photo taken from *Aeroplano "Savoia-Marchetti" Tipo S. 79*, op. cit. in bibliography).

▲ Enamelled metal buttonhole badge, for civilian dress, reproducing the two ribbons relating to the two Bronze Medals for Military Valour, belonging to Carlo Winspeare (author photo).

▼ Eruption of the volcano Vesuvius (1,281 m) seen from an airport at its foot, in the background a 'camouflaged' SAI-MAN 202 (photo taken from https://catalog.archives.gov/).

▲ Another photo of Carlo Winspeare with the rank of Air Force lieutenant sewn onto his flight jacket (photo g.c. Collection Edoardo Winspeare).

▲ An aluminium Air Force lieutenant's rank was sewn onto Carlo Winspeare's flight jacket, as per photographic evidence (author's photo).

▼ An Air Force lieutenant's sleeve rank, embroidered in canvass, was sewn onto Carlo Winspeare's uniform (author photo).

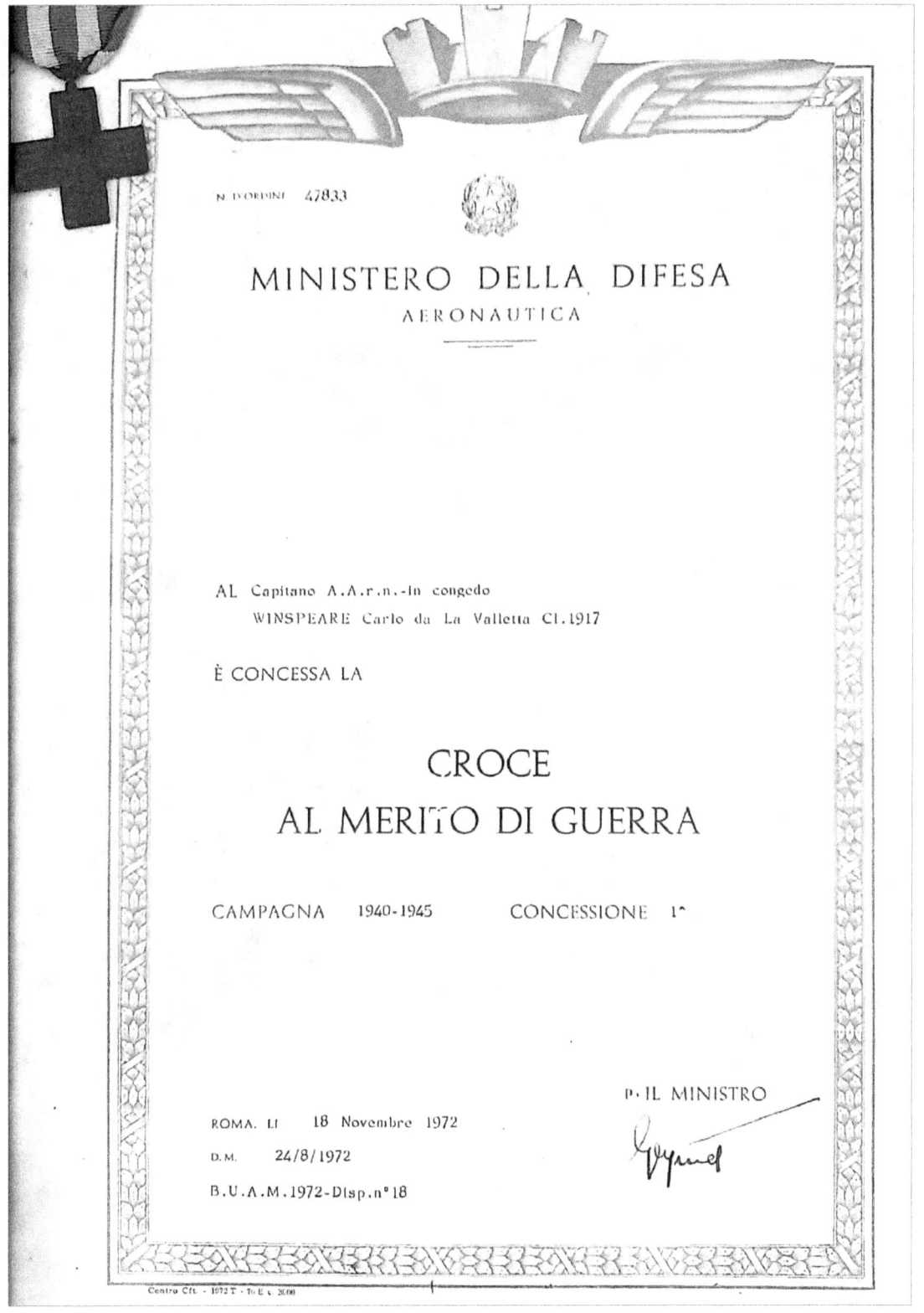

▲ Diploma of the Croce al Merito di Guerra (1st concession) and the relevant medal with which Carlo Winspeare was decorated on 24 August 1972 (photo g.c. Collezione Edoardo Winspeare).

▲ Villa Salve (18th century) on the Vomero hill, where Via S. Stefano, formerly Via Puteolana, once passed for colles, was the Neapolitan home of Carlo Winspeare. During the Second World War, given its strategic position, the villa was requisitioned by the Germans and later by the Allies (Special Corps and 401 Signals). The author was lucky enough to live there (author's photo).

▼ On 11 July 1945 Carlo Winspeare married Donna Maria Vittoria Colonna dei Principi di Stigliano. In the background you can make out part of the Church of Santo Stefano in the residential complex that was owned by the Winspeare family at the time. The clothes worn by the bride and groom, although elegant, show, with their simplicity, the difficult times in which they lived: the war in Europe had only been over for two months and Italy was devastated (photo g.c. Collection Edoardo Winspeare).

> Naples 6-IV-45
>
> The undersigned exposes the following:
> he is the owner of three houses ("Villa Salve", Piazza S. Stefano 6 and Via S. Stefano 4 and 3; this last house is still requisitioned but actually not occupied) requisitioned by Special Corps (Piazza S. Stefano 6) and 401 Signals (Via S. Stefano 3 e 4). As he is obliged by these circumstances to live only in one room, and as he has no room for his work (biological research), he would like to have at least one room derequisitioned in Via S. Stefano 4 and a depot in the same house. The room he would like to be derequisitioned is the last one with the fireplace.
> The name of the C.O. of the unit actually occupying his house is Lt. Colonel H. M. Kirkaldy. Via Tasso 315
> Yours truly
> Dr. Charles Winspeare
> "Villa Salve"
> Via S. Stefano 4
> Naples

▲ Letter from Carlo Winspeare dated 06.04.1945 and addressed to Headquarters, Allied Military Government, Naples, requesting the derequisition of at least one room and a storage room, at "Villa Salve" in via S. Stefano 4, so that he could continue his biological research work. On 21.04.1945, the Allied Military Government replied, regretting that it was currently impossible to derequisition his property (photo ACC, taken from: https://tecadigitaleacs.cultura.gov.it/).

▶ Professor Renato Caccioppoli pictured in the mathematics department (now named in his memory) at the University of Naples 'Federico II'. Carlo Winspeare was his pupil (photo taken from https://commons.wikimedia.org/).

▲ Portrait of Carlo Winspeare in a light blue Regia Aeronautica uniform (photo g.c. Collection Edoardo Winspeare).

Mod. A.   N. 98 del modulario R. A.

REGIA AERONAUTICA
MINISTERO DELL'AERONAUTICA
Ispettorato Leva e Matricola

(a) ~~1ª Div. 2ª Sez.~~

1700238

N. di matricola	N. di ruolo
~~6163~~	~~12~~

(b) **Stato di Servizio**

di **Winspeare Carlo**
figlio di *Edoardo* e di *Laraun Clara*
nato il *13 marzo 1917* a *La Valletta (Malta)*
provincia di
Inscritto nelle liste di leva del Comune di *Napoli* Distretto Militare di *Napoli*
Ha prestato giuramento di fedeltà in *Capodichino* il *23.2.1942*
Ammogliato con la
previa autorizzazione sovrana del

SERVIZI, PROMOZIONI E VARIAZIONI NOMINE - ESONERI - RIABILITAZIONI AL PILOTAGGIO	DATA	Stipendi annui
Soldato di Leva, classe 1917 sottoposto a lui... quale rivedibile classe 1917 e laquale si con... fessa ottomitato. Non rispondere alla chiamata alle armi con la classe 1918	2 Maggio 38	
Chiamato alle armi per effetto della circolare n. 121 del G.M. 1939 e giunto	29 marzo 939	
Ammesso al ritardo del Servizio Militare per ragioni di studio, quale iscritto al 1° anno di facoltà di laurea in applicazione dell'art.113 C.U.	29 marzo 939	
Incorporato nella R. Aeronautica, in qualità di Ambre Allievo Ufficiale Pilota di Complemento		

a) Centro di R. M. o Ente matricolare o Ministero. — b) Nelle copie si aggiunge Copia delle

▲ The first page of Carlo Winspeare's service record, this document was of great importance for reconstructing the affairs of 'ours' (photo g.c. Collection Edoardo Winspeare).

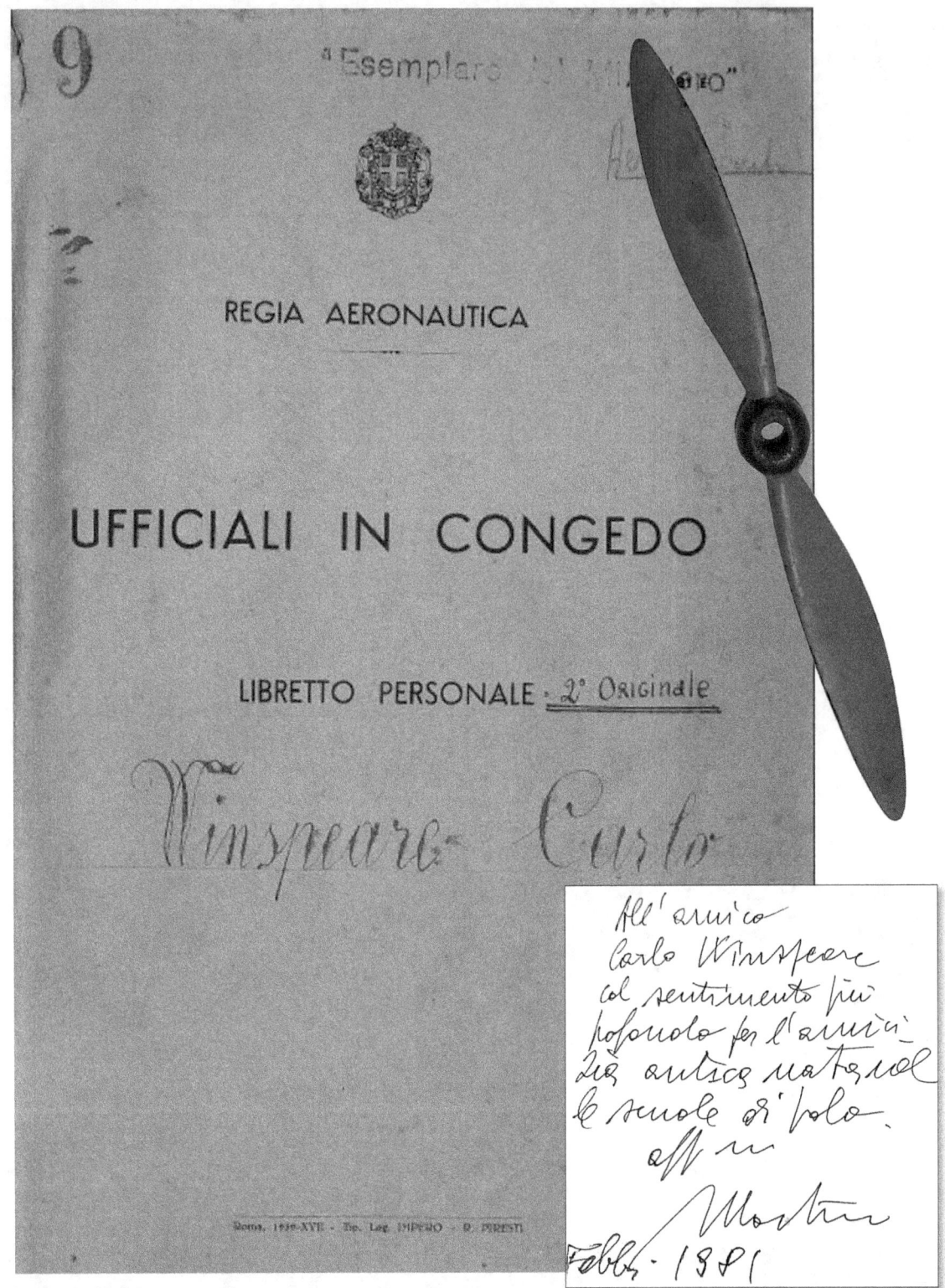

▲ The cover of Carlo Winspeare's personal booklet, which also proved to be fundamental for the reconstruction of the protagonist's adventures (photo g.c. Collezione Edoardo Winspeare). Below: The dedication that Martino Aichner wrote on the copy of his book donated to Carlo Winspeare (author photo).

BIBLIOGRAPHY

Aichner, Martino, *Il Gruppo Buscaglia, Aerosiluranti italiani nella seconda guerra mondiale*, Milano, Ugo Mursia Editore, 1991.

Aichner, Martino – Evangelisti, Giorgio, *Il Gruppo Buscaglia e gli aerosiluranti italiani*, Milano, Longanesi & C., 1972.

Aichner, Martino – Evangelisti, Giorgio, *Storia degli aerosiluranti italiani e del gruppo Buscaglia*, Milano, Longanesi & C., 1969.

Angelucci, Enzo, *Gli Aeroplani*, Milano, Arnoldo Mondadori Editore, 1972.

AA.VV., *Nei Cieli di Guerra, La Regia Aeronautica a colori 1940-45*, Milano, Giorgio Apostolo Editore, 1996.

Biagini, A. – Rainero R. H., (A cura di), *L'Italia in Guerra, Il Terzo Anno - 1942*, Commissione Italiana di Storia Militare, Roma, Stabilimento Grafico Militare Gaeta, 1993.

Bonvicini, Guido, *Carlo Faggioni e gli aerosiluranti italiani*, Milano, Cavallotti Editori, 1987.

Chiocci, Francobaldo, *Gli Affondatori del Cielo*, Roma, Ed. Il Borghese, 1972.

Collegio Araldico, *Libro d'Oro della Nobiltà Italiana*, edizione XXV (2015-2019), Roma, Ettore Gallelli Editore, 2014.

Cuthbert Rexford-Welch, Samuel, *The Royal Air Force Medical Services,* Vol. 3, London, Her Majesty's Stationery Office, 1958.

D'Amico, F., Valentini, G., *Regia Aeronautica*, Vol. 2, Carrollton, Squadron/Signal Publications, 1986.

Fioravanzo, Giuseppe, *Le azioni navali in Mediterraneo, dal 1° aprile 1941 all'8 settembre 1943*, Vol. V della serie "La Marina Italiana nella Seconda Guerra Mondiale", Roma, Ufficio Storico della Marina Militare, 1970.

Hastings, Max, *La Battaglia di mezzo agosto, Operazione Pedestal, 1942: la flotta che salvò Malta*, Vicenza, Neri Pozza Editore, 2023.

Hillgruber, Andreas, (A cura di), *Kriegstagebuch des Oberkommandos der Wehrmacht, (Wehrmachtführungsstab), Band II: 1. Januar 1942 - 31. Dezember 1942*, Frankfurt am Main, Bernard & Graefe Verlag für Wehrwesen, 1963.

Llewellyn-Jones, Malcom, *Operation Pedestal, Convoy to Malta, August 11-15 1942*, s.l., Naval Historical Branch, 2012.

Mattesini, Francesco, *Gli aerosiluranti italiani e tedeschi nella seconda guerra mondiale (1940-1945)*, Vol. 2, Zanica, Soldiershop Publishing, 2022.

Mattesini, Francesco, *La battaglia aeronavale di Mezzo Agosto*, Roma, Edizioni dell'Ateneo, 1986.

Ministero dell'Aeronautica, *Aeroplano "Savoia Marchetti" Tipo S. 79*, Roma, Società Italiana Aeroplani e Idrovolanti "Savoia-Marchetti" Sesto Calende.

Ministero dell'Aeronautica, *Catalogo Nomenclatore per Aeroplano Caproni 313 da Ricognizione e medio Bombardamento*, Milano, Ufficio Pubblicazioni Tecniche della Aeroplani Caproni S. A., 1942.

Ministero della Cultura Popolare, (A cura del), *La Battaglia del Canale di Sicilia, (Mezz'agosto 1942-XX)*, Roma, Istituto Romano di Arti Grafiche, 1942.

Molteni, Mirko, *L'aviazione italiana 1940-1945, Azioni belliche e scelte operative*, Bologna, Odoya, 2018.

Niccoli, Riccardo, *Aerei*, Novara, Istituto Geografico De Agostini, 2000.

Perini, Alessandro, *I diari di Babka, 1943-1944 aristocrazia antifascista e missioni segrete*, s.l., Lulu.com, 2007.

Rogers, Anthony, *Siege of Malta 1940-42*, London, Greenhill Books, 2020.

Roskill, S. W., *The War at Sea 1939-1945, Vol. II, The Period of Balance*, London, J. R. M. Butler, 1956.

Santoro, Giuseppe, *L'Aeronautica italiana nella seconda Guerra mondiale*, Milano-Roma, Edizioni Esse, 1966.

Sponza, Ottone, *Nato per volare*, Milano, Giorgio Apostolo Editore, 1998.

Stato Maggiore della R. Aeronautica, Ufficio Aerosiluranti, *Manuale del silurista di aeronautica*, Roma, Istituto Poligrafico dello Stato, 1942.

Unia, Carlo, *Storia degli Aerosiluranti Italiani*, Roma, Bizzarri, 1974.

Vadalà, Francesco, *L'Aeronautica a Benevento*, Benevento, Edizioni Realtà Sannita, 2009.

Newspaper and magazines

Aerei italiani contro navi inglesi in Supplemento a "Le vie dell'aria", n. 24, 21 giugno, 1942.

Aerosilurante italiano pronto alla partenza in "Stampa Sera", anno 76, n. 181, Torino, giovedì venerdì, 30-31 luglio, 1942.

Alberghini Maltoni, Luciano, *Lo Stormo dei "quattro gatti", l'ultimo stormo bombardieri della Regia Aeronautica* in "Storia Militare", marzo 2002.

Bassi, Mario, *Supremo e disperato sforzo nemico per tentare il rifornimento di Malta* in "La Stampa", anno 76, n. 194, Torino, venerdì, 14 agosto, 1942.

Beltrame, A., (Disegno di) in "La Domenica del Corriere, Supplemento illustrato del Corriere della Sera", anno 44, n. 34, 23 agosto 1942.

Bianchi, Fabio – Maraziti, Antonio, *Gli Aerosiluranti Italiani 1940-1945, I reparti, le macchine, le imprese* in "Storia Militare Dossier", n. 14, maggio - giugno 2014.

Bollettino N. 804 in "il Resto del Carlino", anno 58, n. 191, Bologna, martedì, 11 agosto, 1942.

Bollettino N. 805 in "il Resto del Carlino", anno 58, n. 192, Bologna, mercoledì, 12 agosto, 1942.

Bollettino N. 806 in "Cronache della Guerra", Roma, Anno IV, N. 34, 22 agosto 1942.

Bollettino N. 809 in "Stampa Sera", anno 76, n. 194, Torino, venerdì sabato, 14-15 agosto, 1942.

Bollettino N. 810 in "il Resto del Carlino", anno 58, n. 195, Bologna, lunedì, 17 agosto, 1942.

Caputi, Giuseppe, *La grande vittoria mediterranea nelle acque tunisine* in "Cronache della Guerra", Roma, Anno IV, N. 34, 22 agosto 1942.

"Carry on, Malta!" The Great Convoy Fight in "The Illustrated London News", London, Saturday, August 29, 1942, page 22.

Central Chancery of the Orders of Knighthood in "Third Supplement to The London Gazette of Friday, the 4th of September, 1942", London, His Majesty's Stationery Office, 1942.

Convoy battle: Nazis say more warships hit in "Daily Mirror", London, Friday, August 14, 1942.

Das Mittelmeer bleibt für England gesperrt in "Völkischer Beobachter", 228. Ausg. 55. Jahrg., Wien, Sonntag, 16. August 1942.

Documentario della battaglia aeronavale di mezz'agosto nel Mediterraneo Centrale in "Cronache della Guerra", Roma, Anno IV, N. 36, 5 settembre 1942.

Fiero proclama del Duce ai vittoriosi in "il Resto del Carlino", anno 58, n. 195, Bologna, lunedì, 17 agosto, 1942.

Kayser, von, Bruno, *Stukas über dem Mittelmeer* in "Der Adler", n. 3, Berlino 4 febbraio 1941.

Galea, Albert, *Operation Pedestal: The heroes who helped save Malta from starvation* in "The Malta Independent", Monday, 15 August 2022.

Gli aerosiluranti italiani negli ultimi scontri navali in "La Stampa", anno 76, n. 237, Torino, lunedì, 5 ottobre, 1942.

Il bollettino straordinario N. 808 in "Il Piccolo", Trieste, venerdì, 14 agosto, 1942.

Il convoglio inglese decimato in "Il Piccolo", Trieste, venerdì, 14 agosto, 1942.

I Was There! in "The War Illustrated", n. 137, September 18, 1942.

La battaglia dell'Atlantico in "7 Anni di Guerra, fotostoria del secondo conflitto mondiale visto dalle due parti in lotta", n. 7, 10 Novembre 1963.

L'affondatore della "Eagle" in "Le Ultime Notizie, Il Piccolo delle Ore Diciotto", Trieste, giovedì, 13 agosto, 1942.

L'annientamento del convoglio nemico in "Il Mattino", Napoli, sabato, 15 agosto, 1942.

La portaerei "Eagle„ affondata in "Corriere della Sera", Milano, mercoledì, 12 agosto, 1942.

Le epiche fasi della lotta in "Il Popolo di Trieste, Il Piccolo della Sera", n. 818, Trieste, venerdì, 14 agosto, 1942.

L'eroico comandante Buscaglia in "Tempo", n. 182, Roma, 19-26 novembre 1942.

Macmillan, Norman, *The War In The Air* in "The War Illustrated", n. 136, September 4, 1942.

Macmillan, Norman, *The War In The Air* in "The War Illustrated", n. 137, September 18, 1942.

Maressi, Giovanni, *Landschutz Istria*, 3ª parte in "Fronti di Guerra", Anno 14, n. 81, maggio 2022.

McMurtrie, Francis E., *The War At Sea* in "The War Illustrated", n. 136, September 4, 1942.

Navi in fiamme al largo delle coste tunisine in "Il Messaggero", Roma, sabato, 15 agosto, 1942.

Nessun trasporto scampato alla strage in "La Stampa", anno 76, n. 195, Torino, sabato, 15 agosto, 1942.

Pag. 18, in "Auckland Weekly News", Auckland, Wednesday, 24 March 1943.

Poderoso attacco a un convoglio scortato da un'imponente flotta in "Le Ultime Notizie, Il Piccolo delle ore diciotto", serie n. 7054, Trieste, giovedì, 13 agosto, 1942.

Riesengeleitzug im Mittelmeer zerschlagen in "Völkischer Beobachter", 226. Ausg. 55. Jahrg., Wien, Freitag, 14. August 1942.

Rizza, Claudio, *Breaking Hagelin* in "Rivista Marittima", Novembre, 2019.

Stormi italiani in "Il Mattino Illustrato", anno XVIII, n. 4, Napoli, 27 gennaio - 3 febbraio 1941.

Syfret, Edward Neville, *Operation "Pedestal"* in "Supplement to The London Gazette of Tuesday, the 10th of August, 1948", London, His Majesty's Stationery Office, 1948.

The Malta convoy in "The Sphere", London, Saturday, August 29, 1942, pages 281-283.

Tre navi da guerra e dieci piroscafi colati a picco in "il Resto del Carlino", anno 58, n. 194, Bologna, venerdì, 14 agosto, 1942.

U-Boote versenkten 13 Schiffe mit 86 000 brt in "Marburger Zeitung", Nr. 224, 82. Jahrgang, Marburg-Drau, Mittwoch, 12. August 1942.

Vego, Milan, *Major Convoy Operation to Malta, 10-15 August 1942 (Operation Pedestal)* in "Naval War College Review", Vol. 63, No. 1, Newport, U.S. Naval War College Press, Winter 2010.

Yonay, Ehud, *Top Guns* in "California Magazine", May 1983.

Archival sources

ACS, *Allied Control Commission – ACC*, Naples Zone, Liaison Officer, 195.

Archivio Fotografico, Fondazione Ranieri di Sorbello, immagine di Uguccione Ranieri di Sorbello in tenuta da tenente d'artiglieria (c. 1928).

Archivio Storico Istituto Luce, codice filmato: C027401.

AUSAM, fondo Diari Storici Seconda Guerra Mondiale 1940-1945, Serie anno 1942, fascicolo 897, 132° Gruppo Aerosiluranti, 9-15 agosto 1942.

AUSAM, fondo Documentazione personale, Serie libretti, Libretto personale del pilota Winspeare Carlo.

IWM, Catalogue number UKY 425.

National Archives, Kew, War Office, I.S.9 Progress Reports for November 4–21, 1943, A. Robb, Captain. No. 5 Field Section.

National Archives, Kew, War Cabinet. Chiefs Of Staff Committee. Minutes of Meeting held on Friday, 31st July, 1942, at 10.30 a.m., CAB 79/22/23.

National Archives, Kew, War Cabinet. Chiefs Of Staff Committee. Minutes of Meeting held on Tuesday, 11st August, 1942, at 5.45 p.m., CAB 79/56/86.

Ministero della Difesa, Direzione Generale per il Personale Militare, V Reparto 12ª Divisione, Servizio Orvieto – 3ª Sezione, Stato di servizio di Winspeare Carlo.

Ministero della Difesa, Direzione Generale per il Personale Militare, III Reparto, Servizio Ricompense e Onorificenze, proposta Medaglia di Bronzo al Valor Militare, Winspeare Carlo.

National Museum of the Royal Navy, Admiralty War Diaries, Malta Command, April to December 1942, Diary of Events in the Malta Command from 1st to 31st August 1942.

National Museum of the Royal Navy, Admiralty War Diaries, Mediterranean Fleet, July to September 1942, Mediterranean War Diary, August 1942.

SMA, Ufficio Storico, fondo Memorie storiche 1923-1943, Memoria servizi archivistici, 2012.

Other sources

Bear_EAF51, *Il Martin Baltimore: l'ultimo bombardiere italiano*.
Comune di Napoli, Ufficio dello Stato Civile, registro degli Atti di Matrimonio.
Copello, Massimo, *Il ricordo dei ricordi di un pilota di guerra*, 2010.
Decreto 17 marzo 1949.
Decreto Luogotenenziale 8 maggio 1946.
De Zeng, Henry L. - Stankey, Douglas G., *Luftwaffe Officer Career Summaries 1935-1945*, Version: 01.04.2023.
Fortunato, Francesco, *Fremma Uno: Campo Vesuvio e Stormo Baltimore, dove nasce l'Aeronautica Italiana*, sabato 26 aprile 2014.
Mattesini, Francesco, *Corrispondenza con l'autore del 25 e 26 settembre 2023*.
Regio decreto 4 novembre 1932, n. 1423 *Nuove disposizioni per la concessione delle medaglie e della croce di guerra al valor militare* e successive modificazioni.
Sobatti, Carlo, *Libretto personale di volo, annotazione del 12.08.1942*.
Vermisstenbildlisten, Suchdienst, Deutsches Rotes Kreuz, 1957.
Winspeare, Carlo, *codice fiscale*, WNSCRL17C13Z121L.
Winspeare, Edoardo, *Mio zio, Carlo Winspeare*, 2023.
Winspeare, Edoardo, *Lettera privata all'autore del 9 dicembre 2020*.
Winspeare, Edoardo, *Lettera privata all'autore dell'8 febbraio 2022*.
Winspeare, Edoardo, *Lettera privata all'autore del 27 settembre 2023*.
Winspeare, Riccardo, *Corrispondenza con Maria Vittoria Colonna del 25 luglio 1954*.

Web

www.ww2.dk
www.aircrewremembered.com
www.ancestors.familysearch.org
www.aucklandmuseum.com
www.briancrabbmaritimebooks.co.uk
www.camp59survivors.com
www.conlapelleappesaaunchiodo.blogspot.com
www.cwgc.org
www.difesa.it
www.gavs.it
www.governo.it
www.ibiblio.org
www.istitutodelnastroazzurro.org
www.marina.difesa.it
www.melbournestar.co.uk
www.movm.it
www.nobili-napoletani.it
www.partigianiditalia.cultura.gov.it
www.rafcommands.com
www.regiamarina.net
www.volksbund.de

Aknowledgments

Alegi Gregory, Belli Mauro, Bianchini Enzo, Borrini Massimiliano, Bovino Monica, Brillini Diego, Cocola Paola, De Jeso Genoveffa, Dell'Amico Cesare, Di Cocco Alivernini Marco, Faltoni Giancarlo, Fochesato Bruno, Graziano Vincenzo, Greco Francesco, Hill Dennis, Pragliola Lucio, Raiano Michele, Rallo Michele, Rapolla Venanzio, Rastrelli Paolo, Spurr Brian, Venditti Carlo, Winspeare Edoardo.

TITOLI GIÀ PUBBLICATI - TITLES ALREADY PUBLISHING

www.ingramcontent.com/pod-product-compliance
Lightning Source LLC
LaVergne TN
LVHW081538070526
838199LV00056B/3708